Teaching with Confidence

A guide to enhancing teacher self-esteem

DENIS LAWRENCE

P·C·P
Paul Chapman
Publishing Ltd

Paul Chapman Publishing Ltd
A SAGE Publications Company
6 Bonhill Street
London EC2A 4PU

SAGE Publications Inc
2455 Teller Road
Thousand Oaks, California 91320

SAGE Publications India Pvt Ltd
32, M-Block Market
Greater Kailash -I
New Delhi 110 048

British Library Cataloguing in Publication data

A catalogue record for this book is available from the British Library

ISBN 0-7619-6330-8
ISBN 0-7619-6331-6 (pbk)

Library of Congress catalog card number available

Typeset by Dorwyn Ltd, Rowlands Castle
Printed and bound in Great Britain

Contents

Acknowledgements

I should like to express my thanks to those teachers and head-teachers in England and in Australia who so willingly gave up their valuable time to comment on the material in this book. I am also indebted to them for supplying information regarding the current state of morale in their schools. The impetus for this book came mainly from these people who, for reasons of propriety, must remain anonymous.

Above all, I offer grateful thanks to my wife, Anne, for reading the manuscript and for her valuable suggestions and sustained encouragement throughout.

Preface

Teachers today are, without doubt, under increasing pressures from many sources. Foremost among these pressures has been an increasing workload, mainly the result of numerous government initiatives. This has placed untold pressures on teachers. In a recent survey, commissioned in 1998 by the UK Association of Teachers & Lecturers, 66 per cent of primary teachers felt they no longer had sufficient time to do their job properly, and even more disturbing was that 44 per cent of this group complained of job stress. On top of this, successive governments have blamed them for failing to help children reach some hypothetical standard of attainment. Moreover, these pressures appear to apply not only to teachers in the UK. From recent conversations with a primary school principal and several class teachers in different schools in Australia, it seems that teachers there perceive themselves to be under similar pressures to those experienced by teachers in the UK. They also complain of low staff morale and of receiving regular criticism from government sources.

An additional contributor to the stress in teaching today appears to be the widening of the teacher's role. Their traditional role has gradually changed so that teaching has become one of the 'helping professions', and not solely a profession that educates. Teachers today have to act as if they were psychologists and social workers in addition to being educators, as they are expected to take a major role in helping children develop their personalities. This widening of their role has resulted in other kinds of pressures, such as a vast increase in the amount of paperwork they are expected to do. They are also increasingly being asked to become administrators and accountants. All these new roles bring their own uniquely added strains and stresses.

The media both in the UK and in Australia regularly contain reports of teachers being subjected to criticism both by governments and by parents. In fact, society in general appears to blame teachers for most of its ills. It is hard to resist the view that teaching today is no longer a respected profession in society. Despite this, the typical teacher continues to function gallantly, trying hard to ignore the criticisms of society as well as having to cope with the increasing demands made by governments. Surely the time has come for teachers to begin to consider the effects on them personally of these extra demands and to begin to protect themselves from the inevitable strains involved in being a teacher.

Teachers in general are dedicated professionals who have usually come into the profession for satisfactions other than material rewards. Most teachers could earn higher salaries in other jobs and in other professions. They have chosen to work with children because they genuinely feel they can make a difference to the quality of their lives. But they tend to be a self-effacing lot on the whole, and if the above were voiced in a typical staffroom the chances are that it would be met with an embarrassed silence. The fact remains, however, that teachers in general are dedicated to helping children; in short they are nice people. But it is this very 'niceness' that has made teachers their own worst enemies.

Teacher self-esteem is continuously under threat through these increasing pressures so the need for teachers to look after themselves has never been more urgent. Teaching is still a worthwhile and rewarding profession but even the strongest of teachers will be at risk of burn-out unless they learn how to protect themselves. This book aims not only to alert teachers to what is happening to the profession but also to help them understand how to set about protecting themselves.

Although the book is aimed mainly at serving teachers, many of the strategies outlined are recommended also to student teachers to help them prepare for the harsh realities of the job they will eventually encounter once they enter schools. As such, the book could well be a useful supplement for personal development courses for student teachers in colleges of education.

For those teachers who may wish to become acquainted with the theoretical framework to the strategies outlined, a brief explanation of Self-Concept Theory is presented in the Appendix. While this is not essential reading, again it should prove to be of interest to students in training who may be considering choosing the concept as a research topic.

Introduction

The teaching profession has been held in high regard throughout the ages and rightly recognised by society as a true vocation. Although the financial rewards have never been comparable with those in many other professions, such as medicine, for example, there are other satisfactions to be gained from teaching that have been recognised as more than adequate compensation. The stimulation gained through contact with young enquiring minds and the knowledge that you have been able to help children along the road to becoming responsible adults are particular joys not so easily experienced in other professions.

If these are valid comments, why is it that today we are witnessing a decline in the numbers of young people applying to enter the training institutions? Why is there an increase in the number of teachers applying for early retirement? Why are so many teachers talking of stress and burn-out? The short answer to this is that the teaching profession has suffered a gradual change in so many ways over the last few decades that the job is no longer the happy one it was even a short while ago. Teachers today are under siege. There are many reasons for this state of affairs, but the end product is a general lowering of teacher self-esteem with teachers today more inclined to be cynical about their profession. The worrying decline in the number of people going into the profession is perhaps no surprise in view of the fact that the job has become less attractive.

Despite the added pressures of the job, teaching could once more be the attractive and rewarding profession it used to be if only the profession would begin to care more for itself. Without denying that their first priority should continue to be concern for the welfare of children in their care, it is time now to accept that teachers also have needs. Foremost among these needs is the need for self-esteem. Teachers have always recognised the child's need for self-esteem. There is no denying that the relationship between self-esteem, academic achievement, and the behaviour of children has been one of the most exciting educational research findings of recent times. It is well documented that children with high self-esteem achieve more and have fewer behavioural problems. As a result, most teachers today are well acquainted with the need to enhance children's self-esteem (Lawrence, 1996). If only the same could be said about the need to enhance the teacher's self-esteem. Rarely, if ever, do teachers consider their own self-esteem levels, let alone reflect on the need to enhance them. This is curious, as there is ample research evidence showing that teachers with high self-esteem usually produce children with high self-esteem (Coombs, 1965). The well-known 'modelling effect' described by Bandura, where children tend to copy the behaviour of adults, occurs regularly in teaching, with children identifying with the self-esteem of the teacher (Bandura, 1977). This is a powerful process, especially as the teacher regularly comes into personal contact with the child.

Teachers have a responsibility when they make a relationship with a child, as there are so many opportunities in a classroom day to influence the child's developing personality. This often occurs without teachers being consciously aware of it. Simply by making a relationship with a child, the teacher is affecting the child for good or for ill. It is interesting to try to remember, as adults, the particular teachers whom we liked best when we were at school. Invariably, those we remember as the teachers we liked are those who cared about us and these are also the teachers in whose classes we achieved the most. Once again, there is evidence of the inextricable link between self-esteem and achievement. The self-esteem of the teacher is of paramount importance in this context.

Teachers have always been aware of the importance of the teacher–pupil relationship and the need to develop a good rapport with children. Perhaps in the past this has been mainly an intuitive awareness, but today there is research evidence to show how this rapport affects not only the child's behaviour and personality but also the child's attainments (Lawrence, 1997). There is well-documented research evidence showing a relationship between the quality of the rapport between pupil and teacher and the child's level of self-esteem. This is why training courses these days have units on developing teacher communication skills as an aid to developing children's self-esteem. It is not so easily acknowledged, however, that the teacher with good communication skills is usually the teacher with high self-esteem and it is the development of the teacher's self-esteem which is the key to the process. The value of teachers developing their own self-esteem has yet to be recognised on teacher education courses through specific units on maintaining and enhancing teacher self-esteem, despite the fact that there is a strong case for arguing the merits of such courses. This book could provide some of the material, at least, on a teacher education course.

Enhancing teacher self-esteem is not only desirable in the interests of the child but, perhaps more importantly, it is essential to ensure high teacher self-esteem in order to help teachers cope better with the everyday strains and stresses of teaching. It is probably the case that most schools, at some time or other, have at least one teacher in the staffroom whom others euphemistically describe as 'feeling below par'. This teacher usually receives sympathy from the rest of the staff and it may even be suggested that the teacher take some time off work. Rarely would the real reason for this teacher's condition be identified. The chances are that the inevitable strains of the job have taken their toll and the self-esteem of the teacher now needs attention. The need for teachers to focus on their own self-esteem before reaching this point has usually been ignored. In fact, the situation is often quite the reverse, with teachers deliberately neglecting their own needs in the service of their job. Teachers are notorious for putting in more hours of work over and above those required by their contracts. Perhaps this is because teachers on the whole are caring people and feel their reward is in doing their best for the children in their care. Why else would they enter such a demanding profession with its relatively meagre financial rewards and regular criticism from outside the profession?

Traditionally it has been said that being involved in helping children develop and achieve is sufficient reward in itself. The fact is, however, that most teachers today are not always as free to become involved in the welfare and education of children as they were in the past. The job has become many-sided and the pressures on teachers have steadily increased, so that today teachers are not able to spend as much time with individual children as they did in the past. These extra demands have put tremendous strains on teachers. It is not surprising that the job is now regarded as a high-risk profession in respect of stress.

Many factors are responsible for the rise in teacher stress. One factor is that the job is changing at a rapid rate. Teachers are now expected to be managers as well as teachers, and with increasing administrative demands from local and central government, many teachers today are beginning to question what they perceive to be an ambiguous and, in some cases, an impossible role. As the job changes, some teachers are even wondering whether they made the right choice to enter the profession in the first place. Requests for early retirement are not uncommon. Moreover, there is some evidence that the incidence of stress in the teaching profession is steadily on the increase. Once again, there is need to consider teacher self-esteem, as there appears to be a relationship between teacher stress and self-esteem. It is obvious that people under stress inevitably perform less efficiently, and sooner or later their confidence goes. As teachers with low self-esteem tend to produce children with low self-esteem, a vicious circle is soon set up. Children with low self-esteem show more problems and achieve less; this in turn puts teachers under more stress and so self-esteem drops even further.

The message is clear. Teachers today need guidance on how to care more for themselves and be shown how to focus more on the satisfaction of their own psychological needs if they are to continue to carry out their role effectively. It is not only that in so doing they will be able to cope better with the stresses of teaching, but also they will be fitter physically. There is an accumulating body of research evidence showing a relationship between a happy personality and the body's immune system. In other words, unhappy teachers may be more likely to pick up infections and to become ill, so unless they learn how to nurture themselves as well as their pupils they will put their own health at risk as well as risking the welfare of their pupils. The self-esteem of the teacher holds the key to all this. If we can help teachers with their own self-esteem, they will become happier and healthier people and more effective teachers; the end result being happier children with higher attainments.

There are a multitude of factors contributing to a person's level of self-esteem, beginning at birth and continuing throughout life. By the time a person is a fully-fledged adult they have been subjected to numerous influences, negative and positive. Some teachers probably enter the profession already with low self-esteem, whilst there are others, probably the majority, who begin confidently enough but then gradually develop low self-esteem as the pressures of the job increase, as discussed above. It is important to emphasise that even where there may have been negative influences which have contributed to low self-esteem, these are in the past and need no longer motivate. Although the present personality is a result of these influences, combined with inherited factors, counselling research has shown how we can start with the here-and-now and change *now* provided we are prepared to put in the effort. No matter what the reasons for the development of low self-esteem may be, people can change. The process of changing a person's personality used to imply a lengthy course of counselling or psychotherapy. We know now that this is not necessary, particularly where the aim is simply to change self-esteem and help people to become more confident. After all, we are talking here of teachers who originally set out in teaching as healthy and confident; we are not talking of people who have deep-rooted personality disorders and who probably do need more skilled help from psychiatric practitioners. The approach outlined in this book is aimed at teachers who are normal and healthy, but who may have begun to lose confidence in themselves as a result of the inevitable stresses of the job. These are the people who so often refuse to accept that they need help and certainly would not think of considering that they needed psychiatric help. This attitude is common and in most cases is probably the correct one. These teachers simply need to be shown how to help themselves, and this book sets out to show how they can do this through a self-help course involving the adoption of specific strategies. The exercises and strategies outlined should prove to be of invaluable help to teachers who are prepared to devote the necessary time to the activities and to consider using the strategies. The rewards will be well worth the effort demanded.

The material in the book is based on valid research as well as on the author's own experience as a teacher, psychologist and lecturer in teacher education in the UK and in Australia. *Teaching with Confidence* should prove to be of value not only as a practical guide for teachers to enhance their self-esteem but also as a reference book for students of self-esteem, as it also presents a useful summary of the history and development of the Self-Concept Theory in the Appendix. This section should also be useful for those teachers who may wish to know more about the theoretical framework to the practical strategies outlined.

A number of questions are posed at the end of each chapter, together with a summary of the chapter's main points. These are included to increase further the reader's understanding of the material presented. They are supplemented by an appropriate activity, and a short list of books, purposely selected for those who may wish to read of the concepts in more depth.

The book begins with a chapter on how to assess the main personality traits. The reader should not be too concerned if their scores on these tests are not quite those they had anticipated. Almost certainly these scores will change when the questionnaires are taken a second time after having completed the book together with the various strategies suggested throughout.

Chapter 1

Assessing personal characteristics

As people develop and mature, they gradually become more aware of themselves and the sort of people they have become. We can say that people become more conscious of themselves. This process is known as developing a self-image and happens gradually as we go through life taking in numerous experiences. Learning about ourselves is one of life's challenges and consists of the discovery of some things we like about ourselves and some other things we may not be so happy about.

Normally we try to change the things we don't like about ourselves. Although there will be some characteristics that are resistant to change, on the whole the evidence is that we can change the things we don't like. Some of our characteristics we are not happy about may be those most resistant to change. For instance, we may not like being highly emotional. The research would indicate that emotionality is a constitutional factor and therefore resistant to change. Even so, we can learn how to accept this trait in our personality and learn strategies to help us live with it so that it is no longer a problem to us. Before being able to set about changing any aspects of our personality it is necessary first to be aware of our unique personality traits. The questionnaires presented in this chapter might be regarded as a method of accelerating this process of awareness.

As a first step in getting to know yourself it is suggested that you measure your level of self-esteem. The term 'self-esteem' has had many different definitions since it first became an object of study for the psychologist. However, most research workers would now give it a very precise theoretical definition, i.e. *the evaluation of the discrepancy between self-image and ideal self.* A

1

theoretical discussion of Self-Concept Theory is presented in the Appendix. For practical purposes, however, self-esteem can be simply defined as 'confidence'. This is expressed in our abilities and also in our personalities.

Confidence

In an attempt to measure the self-esteem of an individual, a set of questions describing confident behaviour had to be devised. This questionnaire became known as the Lawrence Confidence Scale and was given to a random population in order to establish norms. The **Teacher Confidence Scale** (TECON) is based on the Lawrence Confidence Scale, having been specifically adapted for teachers. You should begin the process of self-awareness by completing the TECON opposite.

Most teachers score between 25 and 35 on the TECON. If you make a score below this average range you should not be discouraged, as no matter what your score you have the knowledge now to set your own targets for improvement. After scoring the questionnaire, consider your responses to the individual questions and identify the areas in your teaching where some improvement may appear to be indicated. As you work through the book you will find strategies and discussions on how best to achieve your target in these specific areas.

Other personality characteristics

'I don't know what it is but I don't seem to be able to get on with that child.'

This comment was heard in a staffroom and is not unusual. Sooner or later most teachers will come across a child, or even perhaps a colleague, whom they find it difficult to get on with for no obvious reason. This does not refer to differences of opinion or conflicts which occur from time to time between most people over specific issues, but refers rather to those more vague conflict situations when we find ourselves saying things like, 'I just don't seem able to get on their wavelength.' This is not to say that kind of situation may not eventually escalate into a full-blown row unless it is resolved. In general, when this happens most of us would simply dismiss the friction and get on with the task at hand. The person with low self-esteem, however, is more

	Yes	No	Don't know

1. There are lots of things in my teaching style I do not like.
2. I often worry about things I have said in the classroom.
3. I often wake at nights worrying about school.
4. I often wish I were in a different job.
5. I hate having to ask colleagues for help.
6. I often feel that students are laughing at me.
7. I do not easily get over it if colleagues find fault with me.
8. I prefer to avoid staff meetings in case I make a fool of myself.
9. I feel that many students dislike me.
10. I worry a lot about mistakes I have made in the past.
11. I give in easily when faced with students who are difficult.
12. I dislike the sound of my voice in the classroom.
13. I feel that other teachers do lots of things better than I do.
14. I usually feel anxious when having to meet a new class.
15. I am not as good as other teachers in organising a classroom.
16. I become easily embarrassed when criticised in the staffroom.
17. I feel threatened by parents.
18. I worry about my appearance.
19. Other teachers are more popular than I am.
20. I find it hard to make decisions.

Score: 2 points for No, 1 point for Don't know, 0 for Yes.

Teacher confidence scale (TECON)

likely to take it personally and even to blame themselves as being the cause of the problem. So why do these problems occur and who is responsible for them? The short answer is that this is an example of what is known as a 'clash of personalities' based on differences in innate temperament. A knowledge of individual differences of temperament in people can help us understand what is happening here.

Academics over the years have argued over how much of personality is inherited and how much is learned. The old 'nature/nurture' debate continues to rage with regard to abilities but a consensus appears now to have emerged with regard to temperament or personality traits. It seems that there are two dimensions of personality which are there at the beginning and which show very little change throughout life. These are the **introvert/extravert** dimension and the **emotionality** dimension. Both these appear to be normally distributed in the population. People who differ widely on these characteristics perceive the world in different ways and also react emotionally very differently to it. However, armed with a knowledge of our own ratings on these dimensions we are better able to understand not only ourselves but also why clashes of personality can occur. The dimensions are explained below.

Introversion/extraversion

These terms were first introduced by Carl Jung at the beginning of the century. Since then H. Eysenck, R. B. Cattell and other eminent researchers have put this dimension of personality on an experimental basis and shown how it is possible to measure introversion/extraversion. Moreover, there is ample evidence from their research to suggest that introversion/extraversion is an inherited dimension of personality and changes very little throughout life. Before showing how to measure it, let us first define it and show how it affects us in everyday life.

Some people appear to prefer quiet pursuits and are generally quiet people in contrast to others who are noisier and at social events are often described as being the life and soul of the party. The former we call introverts and the latter the extraverts. Whilst extremes on these dimensions do exist, as with most human characteristics, people are generally a bit of each and in the middle of the continuum. An interesting question, of course, is whether we can change our personalities along these dimensions or whether they are fixed from birth. For most of us, all this is a bit academic and presents no real problems in life. However, for those at the extremes, the marked introvert or the marked extravert, there is usually pressure from society to change. Introverts are forever being encouraged to speak up and there is a tendency for extraverts to be told to shut up! The question of whether it is possible to change one's personality type can therefore be a very real conundrum for some people.

The short answer to this question is that the research suggests that this dimension of personality is inherited and does not change much throughout life. One of the most readily available sources of reference for these conclusions is the research conducted over the last 40 years by Hans Eysenck (1997) and his contemporaries. From this research, mainly amongst identical twins reared apart but also from longitudinal studies, there is clear evidence for this dimension being constitutionally determined and probably inherited. Introversion and extraversion can be observed almost from birth when some infants are seen to kick and thrash about in the cot more than others. Moreover, it is seen to be consistent throughout childhood into adult life. If this personality characteristic is inherited the evidence is that all other personality characteristics are learned and expressed in terms of this one. This is why it has been described as being the 'skeleton of personality'.

There is another source of reference from the research pointing to the introvert/extravert dimension being inherited and which shows also that there is likely to be a physiological basis for it. This is the fact that EEG studies, which measure the electrical brain impulses, show radically different alpha and beta wave patterns between introverts and extraverts. Those of the former are low in amplitude and close together whilst those of the latter are high in amplitude and more widely spaced. The significance of this is that wave brain patterns which are low in amplitude indicate that the cortex is understimulated whilst the opposite is true of the wave patterns showing high amplitude. Therefore, on the principle of homeostasis, or an organism's need to maintain a balance between all its systems, the person with the understimulated cortex, i.e. the extravert, feels restless and needs excitement, and so is inclined to be noisy; the introvert, on the other hand, has a cortex which is already highly stimulated and so prefers to be quiet. The practical significance for the teacher of these very different types of personality can easily be appreciated. Children who are at the extremes on this continuum will need different kinds of management in the classroom. However, our concern here is with the *teacher's* personality, although similar principles apply.

As previously stated, one source of stress in teaching can be a difficulty in getting on with some colleagues in the staffroom. This sometimes can be traced to the phenomenon of different personality types. Many misunderstandings can occur simply because of different types perceiving the world in general in different terms. In the first place, the evidence is that people get on better with those of a similar personality to themselves. Opposites do not easily understand each other's point of view; this can lead to an uneasy relationship and even to open conflict. Somewhat amusingly, introverts and extraverts say similar things about each other but distrust each other for opposite reasons. Introverts can be heard to express the view, 'Wouldn't trust that person – hail-fellow, well-met; shallow personality.' Extraverts would say, 'Wouldn't trust that person – still waters run deep; don't know what they are thinking.'

We can now begin to see why teachers should become aware of their basic personality type. This is useful knowledge in their search for a lifestyle which is in keeping with their basic temperament. Teachers, for instance, are more than likely to find their jobs stressful if by temperament they are introverted. Teaching is, after all, an extraverted profession and people who are happiest with their own company would not find it easy operating in a group. This is not to say that introverts should never become teachers; although in general teachers operate in a group situation, there are some successful introverted teachers who have been able to obtain a one-to-one teaching role more suited to their personality type.

Given a knowledge of their own personality type, teachers would be in a much stronger position not only to understand themselves, but also the children in their care as well as their colleagues. The questionnaire opposite should help in this understanding. Place a tick under the most likely response.

Emotionality

'I don't know why but I always have to be careful what I say to that person. I don't know! Some people are so quick to fly off the handle for no reason at all, it seems to me.'

Once again, an expression such as this can mean a personality clash. This time the reference is to differences in emotional

	Always	Sometimes	Never
1. Do you become bored easily?			
2. Would you be unhappy having to spend a whole day alone?			
3. Do you like to have dinner with a lot of friends?			
4. Do you like to talk to other people while shopping?			
5. Do you like lively parties?			
6. Do you like to go on holidays with lots of people?			
7. Do you speak first when meeting people?			
8. Would you enjoy talking to a large group?			
9. Would you prefer visiting a shop rather than ordering goods by phone?			
10. Do you try to vary the kind of clothes you wear?			

Calculate your score as follows:
Always = 2 points   Sometimes = 1 point   Never = 0 points

Scores between 0 and 5 = markedly introverted
Scores between 5 and 15 = average
Scores between 15 and 20 - markedly extraverted

Introvert/extravert scale

expression. The knowledge that people do differ widely on an emotional dimension helps to understand people and their reactions much better.

Emotionality is the second dimension of personality, along with the introversion/extraversion continuum, which Eysenck and his associates have shown to be a basic personality trait and also probably of genetic origin. Emotionality is the extent to which people experience feelings. As with the intro/extravert dimension people can be measured along a continuum with the highly emotional at one end, highly unemotional people at the other, and most people in the middle. Those at the highly emotional end of the continuum are highly sensitive and easily upset, whereas those at the other end are relatively placid in emotional expression and appear to take life as it comes without too many signs of stress.

It can be appreciated how the highly emotional person is their own worst enemy. The highly emotional teacher, for example, is likely to take it personally if a child is uncooperative and so become upset out of all proportion to the actual incident. In the staffroom, where good-natured banter between staff is commonplace, this kind of person would not so easily be able to put up with this without taking offence. Others would then be inclined to regard them as difficult. If this happens they would eventually begin to feel inadequate and low self-esteem would soon follow.

Happily, the highly emotional person need not always be at the prey of their emotions. Once they have recognised their temperament they are in a position to control *it* rather than letting *it* control *them*. As soon as they feel themselves becoming upset they should immediately remind themselves that their reaction may be over the top; they should then count up to ten before reacting. With practice this can soon become automatic.

It may seem from the above discussion that the ideal state would be to be on the low emotionality end of this continuum. However, this can also have its problems. The teacher who is low on emotional expression may not easily be able to empathise with other people. Consequently, they are not going to be quite so sensitive as their more emotional colleagues and may miss opportunities for helping pupils as a result. As they are less sensitive to others' needs, they soon develop a reputation for being 'hard'. Once again, all is not lost, as it is possible for people at this end of the emotional continuum to learn how to become more sensitive. Although initially lacking in their ability to empathise with other people, it is possible for them to develop the capacity of empathy through practice in reflective listening. This is discussed further in Chapter 4 under communication skills.

Whether of high or low emotional expression, the important thing is to be comfortable with your unique personality. We do not always have to change ourselves. It is of far greater importance to be able to understand ourselves.

The questionnaire opposite should help you assess your position on the emotionality continuum.

Final thoughts on assessing personality

It could be argued that the more personality characteristics measured, the greater the insight gained. However, for the purpose

	Always	Sometimes	Never

1. Do other people say you are a moody person?
2. Do you lie awake at nights worrying about things?
3. Do you worry that you might develop a serious illness?
4. Would you be upset if a shopkeeper were rude to you?
5. Do you cry when witnessing a tender scene on TV?
6. Would you cry if you saw an animal destroyed?
7. Do you cry when listening to music?
8. Would you be angry if somebody stepped on your foot accidentally?
9. Do other people say that you have a temper?
10. Do you have nightmares?

Calculate your score as follows:
Always = 2 points   Sometimes = 1 point   Never = 0

Add together your scores:
Scores between 0 and 5 = low emotionality
Scores between 6 and 12 = average emotionality
Scores between 13 and 20 = high emotionality

Emotionality questionnaire

of enhancing teacher self-esteem, an awareness of introversion/ extraversion and emotionality, together with an assessment of present self-esteem levels, will be sufficient foundations on which to build the teacher's self-esteem.

Now that you have got to know more about yourself you are in a stronger position to move on and learn positive skills to enhance your self-esteem. Before developing particular strategies to do this it is necessary first to be aware of the numerous threats to self-esteem that regularly occur in teaching. These are discussed in the next chapter.

Summary

This chapter introduced the reader to the Teacher Confidence Scale which was described as 'self-esteem in action'. The chapter also outlined the main personality characteristics in people which have been described as the 'skeleton of personality'; these are the two dimensions known as introversion/extraversion and emotionality. Questionnaires for the measurement of these two dimensions are included.

Revision questions

1. Why do some people find it difficult to get on with some of their colleagues?
2. What are the main personality characteristics considered to be of genetic origin?
3. What evidence is there for their genetic origin?

Activity

Seek the cooperation of a colleague and assess each other's personality characteristics, first on an intuitive level and then using the questionnaires presented in this chapter.

Further reading

Burns, R. (1979) *The Self-Concept: Theory, Measurement, Development & Behaviour.* Longman: London.
Eysenck, H. (1977) *Psychology Is About People.* Penguin Books: Harmondsworth.

Chapter 2

Threats to self-esteem

_____

'Sometimes I feel so inadequate that I think teaching is not for me after all.'

This statement, heard in a staffroom, is not as unusual as it may seem and is an indication that the teacher who said this is in danger of developing low self-esteem. There are countless situations in teaching that are potential risks to self-esteem. These range from the risks involved in day-to-day relationships with children and colleagues to increased stress levels brought on by the demands of the job. If teachers can be helped to become aware of these potential threatening situations, they can then devise strategies to deal with them and in some cases learn how to prevent them occurring in the first place. The main threats to self-esteem in teaching are discussed below.

Finding the right gradient

'I sometimes feel that I need another challenge in my job, with more responsibility.'

The above statement is not uncommon, particularly amongst teachers who have extended their skills through further study and justifiably would like promotion. They need another challenge.

In order to lead a full and satisfying life, people should present themselves with the right kind of challenge. This challenge should not be too daunting so that failure is inevitable, but neither should it be too easy and so no challenge at all. This process could be called 'finding the right gradient' – rather like climbing a hill. For most people, a 60 per cent gradient would be too steep to climb at any speed and a gentler incline would be preferred.

11

For others this might well present an interesting challenge and success would not be too difficult to achieve. To carry the analogy further and into the teaching profession, some teachers are quite content to remain a class teacher where they are perhaps receiving a sufficiently strong challenge and feel satisfaction. This might not suit others who might become bored after a few years of class teaching and feel that they are not developing to their full potential. This sometimes happens where a teacher has widened their horizons through further study which may have led to another degree – they might feel that they are now ready for the challenge of promotion to a post with more responsibility which the former teacher might find too stressful.

Self-knowledge is the starting point in the quest to find the correct gradient in life. This is another reason for the value of the questionnaires presented in the previous chapter.

Am I in the right profession?

'I sometimes wonder if I am really cut out to be a teacher.'
There is nothing more guaranteed to lower self-esteem than to be engaged in a job day in and day out and believing that you are no good at it. Sadly, experience has shown that there are many teachers who go through this stage of self-doubt and many among this group eventually resign after convincing themselves that they are in the wrong job. Whilst it is perfectly possible that some teachers have indeed chosen the wrong profession and are not suited to it, many more teachers go through this stage of self-doubt unnecessarily. It is a fact of life that we all at some stage doubt our capabilities to some extent, no matter what our job.

One reason for this self-doubt among some teachers stems from the fact that teaching is an extraverted profession on the whole and if they are introverts they are likely to experience undue emotional strain. There is research evidence to indicate that most teachers are extraverts and enjoy the company of people. The majority of readers of this book are likely to have scored towards the extraverted end of the introvert/extravert scale in the last chapter. So, it is not surprising that the popular perception of the teacher in the classroom is one of a marked extravert directing a class of children, in a dominant role, usually with a loud voice. Whilst this may often be true, it is not always the case.

Some successful teachers are quiet introverts, and the chances are that they have been able to obtain a post involving small group teaching. There are also teachers who are introverted and who have not been able to find a post which suits their personalities. Initially they may have been attracted to the profession out of a dedicated desire to help children without having given thought to the fact that they would have to operate in the company of large groups of people. They would find it stressful to have to discipline large groups of children, for example. Teaching, for them, soon becomes a chore and their self-esteem begins to suffer as they begin to doubt their suitability for the job. The temptation to look for a job in a less extraverted role has probably crossed their minds on several occasions. The message to these teachers is first not to give up without reflecting on their original motives for becoming a teacher. If the original motives still exist then they should decide to continue, but recognise that they need to choose an aspect of teaching which caters for their introversion. There are many successful teachers who are happiest in small group work, for instance.

It is important to be sure of the original motive for becoming a teacher. If the real reasons were unconnected to the welfare of children, e.g. short hours, long holidays, then it would be wise to recognise a basic unsuitability for the job and resign. If on the other hand it was out of a genuine need to help children, and they remain committed to children's welfare, then there is no reason why they should not learn how to cope, despite their quieter personality. It is equally important for this type of person to recognise that they will never be the life and soul of the party, but also to recognise that this does not imply a value judgement and that they are a lesser person for all that. There is no relationship between introversion/extraversion and mental health; in other words, there are just as many healthy introverts as there are healthy extraverts. Personality is unique, and the terms introversion and extraversion refer to styles of behaviour that are natural to each person's unique personality.

Parents' evenings

'Not another parents' evening! These things can be so stressful.'

A necessary and usually productive part of the job is

discussing a child's progress with the parents. This takes place in most schools on a pre-arranged parents' open evening. These events are usually pleasant and parents are generally cooperative. After all, they are there because they wish to discuss the progress of their child and so mostly these evenings pass happily enough. On the other hand, there is the occasional parent who can be quite challenging to a teacher. These may be those parents who have preconceived, and sometimes unrealistic, views of their child that make communication with them difficult. Often these parents may be critical of the teacher and of the school in general.

The experienced teacher has learned to recognise this kind of communication difficulty and not to react personally. Such a teacher recognises that these parents often require more time and in-depth discussion of their shared concerns before being able to come to a satisfactory resolution to the perceived conflict. Such a resolution may be needed before the children can receive help. This is one of those instances when teachers may have to act the role of counsellors. Sometimes the complexities of these cases are such that only a trained counsellor can help resolve the issues. Unless this process is understood and teachers learn not to react personally to parental criticism the experience can be very undermining and present a real threat to the teacher's self-esteem. It can be particularly difficult for a new teacher where the child in question may have made little progress and, in addition, may also have a behavioural problem.

In order to prevent such an experience from affecting the teacher's self-esteem it is important to be prepared for it – to be forewarned is to be forearmed. The following transcripts have been selected to illustrate the different ways the low self-esteem teacher and the high self-esteem teacher might conduct an interview with a critical parent.

Low self-esteem teacher

Teacher Good evening, Mr Smith. Sit down. I have a few things to discuss with you.

Parent I hope that does not mean that Jamie has not done well this term.

Teacher I wish I could say that he has done well, but I can't. He has been so naughty that his work has been terrible. His mind is just not on it. What's he like at home?

Parent We have no trouble with him at home; he's a good boy and very helpful.

Teacher I find that hard to believe. You should see him here. He's a thorough nuisance.

Parent It doesn't sound like Jamie. He does say that he thinks you do not like him.

Teacher [getting irritated] I don't like him! How can anybody like him when he's like that?

Parent Well, it seems funny to me that he is no trouble at home and yet he's a nuisance here. I don't think you understand Jamie.

Teacher Are you saying that it's the school's fault?

Parent Well, yes, it makes you wonder. I just think … [interrupted]

Teacher Look here! We fall over backwards to help children in this school but if they don't behave how can we teach them? Jamie is going to have to pull up his socks.

Parent By the way you are talking, I am convinced that Jamie is in the wrong school.

Teacher [decidedly irritated] And I don't think you know your child very well either.

Parent I think perhaps I'll take him to another school if that's your attitude.

[Interview terminated with parent and teacher both angry]

Comments
- Teacher was ill at ease right at the start and so was not appropriately welcoming;
- Teacher quickly took offence and felt threatened by the parent's criticism;
- Teacher was quick to lay blame and did not demonstrate respect for the parent;
- Teacher did not allow the parent to suggest ideas for solving the situation;
- Teacher did not give parent opportunity to express his feelings;

- Teacher and parent 'lost face' and self-esteem was reduced for both.

High self-esteem teacher

Teacher Good evening, Mr Smith. Please sit down. Thank you for coming, especially on such a wet night as this.

Parent Yes. It's raining hard, but I like to know how Jamie is getting on at school.

Teacher I wish I could give you good news, but I'm afraid we have a problem.

Parent Why? What has he been up to?

Teacher Well, several teachers have complained that their lessons are regularly interrupted by Jamie needing to talk to his mates while they are talking and refusing to be quiet even when asked. I wondered if you had any ideas why he might be doing that?

Parent It doesn't sound like Jamie. Do you think he is happy in school? He has said that he thinks you don't like him. I think that it could be your fault.

Teacher I'm sorry to hear that. We do try to ensure that children are happy. Has he said why he thinks I don't like him? If I can find that out perhaps I could do something different.

Parent He says that you are always picking on him.

Teacher Well, I suppose that's partly true really as I'm always having to ask him to be quiet. So I do find it hard to show I like him. I wonder what we can do about that. Do you have any suggestions? I always believe that parents know their children best.

Parent I'll have a strong word with him at home. Do you think he could be bored?

Teacher It's possible he is bored. Does he have any particular hobbies at home?

Parent He's mad about football! That's all he talks about from morning to night.

Teacher Thanks for telling me that. I have an idea that I might be able to get through to him after all. I could suggest extra time on the football field in exchange for being quiet in class.

Parent   Sounds like a good idea to me. And I'll speak to him at home about this.

Teacher Well, thanks again for coming. It's been a useful chat. Perhaps we could meet again in a fortnight to review the situation.

Parent   Yes. I think I'd like to do that. And thank you for giving me your time. Goodbye.

Comments
- Teacher was welcoming and friendly, putting parent at ease;
- Emphasis was on 'problem situation', not on 'problem child';
- Parent was given opportunity to contribute to the remedial plan;
- Parent was given opportunity to express his feelings and given respect;
- Teacher did not take parent's irritation personally;
- Self-esteem was maintained in both teacher and parent.

Many teachers find it useful to have a prepared format for a parents evening for discussing children with their parents. The following points are suggested to assist in this:

- Have a written description of the child's behaviour and/or academic progress with a copy for the parents, and read it together. This should be an objective account without interpretation.
- Be prepared for the parents to deny the behaviour and possibly to react with aggression. Allow them to raise their objections and to express their feelings without interruption. When they have finished, make a comment which communicates that you understand how they feel. This process is called 'active listening'.
- Do not focus on the *child* but rather focus on the *problem situation*, e.g. 'We have a problem situation here as there has been too much talking out of turn in the classroom.'
- Ask if they have any ideas for solving it; then give your own ideas for a solution.
- Offer to try both ways; if they do not agree, explain to them, quietly, that the child is your responsibility while in the classroom.

The exact details of such an interview will, of course, vary from case to case, but by following the above suggestions the teacher should be able to remain clear and focused. The aim is not to be drawn into an emotional argument, and to recognise that the parents themselves also want to have their say.

It can be emotionally draining for a teacher to be confronted by parents, and so it is important to take time to unwind before seeing the next one. After a difficult interview, the teacher should try to sit quietly and remind herself or himself that they are the professionals and are trying to do what is best for the child in the classroom. It may be helpful after the evening to discuss these interviews with a senior colleague. This would not only give the teacher emotional support but on a practical level such a discussion might indicate that more interviews may be needed to help the family further.

The newly qualified teacher

'But I don't feel like a teacher!' – a comment made by a student after the first teaching practice session.

Several surveys amongst students in teaching, and similarly in medicine, have revealed just how insecure students feel when out on their first 'field practice'. It can be a daunting experience the first time student teachers find themselves in front of a whole class of children. Most survive this unscathed, having been well prepared for it, but a few with more vulnerable personalities can suffer agonies. It is essential that all students recognise that it is normal to feel anxious and insecure to some degree the first time they have to give a lesson. The very act of taking on a new job and a new role in any walk of life is sufficient to be a potential threat to self-esteem.

Whenever we are expected to behave or to act in a new way for the first time there is always the tendency to feel anxious or, at the very least, apprehensive. It is a human foible to feel more secure behaving in ways which are familiar to us. The young, newly qualified teacher is particularly at risk in this respect having only too recently been a student, probably with very little or no responsibility for other people. Suddenly, the student is in charge of the welfare of a group of children together with all the expectations that go with the new role of teacher. An adjustment in attitude is demanded as their role changes from that of a student to one of a teacher. The expectations placed on teachers are radically different from those placed on students.

The self-perceptions of teachers are not much different when they take up their first appointments, as the *self* is resistant to change. It *will* change with experience, but this is a gradual process. Once again, to be forewarned is to be forearmed; new teachers need to accept that some apprehension is normal at first and that gradually they will 'feel like teachers' as their experience grows. In addition to their own experiences, the expectations and attitudes of others can hasten the process of change: for example, if the senior teachers in the school also recognise the problem and are willing to give regular support. In any new profession eventually most people grow into the job.

Coping with difficult children

Unfortunately, many training courses do not have a good record in this respect. Traditionally very little emphasis has been given to the need for training in class control. Being in charge of a group of healthy children and having also to help them learn is a difficult task even for the most experienced teacher. Most people would find this difficult to appreciate without having been a teacher.

The need for teachers to be properly equipped with a knowledge of class control strategies and appropriate methods of discipline cannot be sufficiently emphasised. Where this has not been forthcoming during initial training, it should be the responsibility of the head of the school to ensure that all teachers in that school have opportunity to attend in-service courses on the topic. Unfortunately, many teachers are led to believe that difficulty in class control is the result of some kind of character defect on their part. I met this attitude while working as an educational psychologist conducting a small survey with the aim of improving service to schools. I had asked teachers if they would like to fill in a questionnaire recording the number of incidents of difficult behaviour presented in one week's teaching. Out of 20 schools surveyed and 200 questionnaires completed only three teachers admitted to having any difficult children or to any specific incidents. On a follow-up survey involving personal sampling of these respondents it became clear that they all had problems in this area to varying degrees, but did not want this information on record. Judging from their comments it seemed that to admit to having difficult children and to having problems coping with difficult behaviour was regarded by these teachers as a weakness bordering on a character defect. A teacher with high self-esteem would have no difficulty with admitting to having a problem.

Contact with immature minds

'Some teachers become like the kids they teach!'

This statement had been made in a Child Guidance Clinic by parents of a child who had been referred to the Clinic because of behavioural difficulties in the classroom. The comment may have been a reflection of their frustration with the school and possibly also with themselves, but it does raise an important issue. These parents seemed to recognise that regular and prolonged contact with immature minds has the potential for an adverse affect on an adult. It is notable how most parents are glad to see another adult again when their partner returns home from work after they have had to spend all day with their offspring. 'It is good to have an adult conversation again.' It is not only that an adult who spends a length of time with children misses adult conversation; the danger is that there is always the risk of the adult identifying with the child. Emotions are infectious and most young children express emotions in a very intense way. In the classroom, the teacher is not only in contact with young minds but also with immature emotions. If a child displays anger, immediately there is the tendency for the adult in charge to feel the same emotion. Usually, of course, the adult is well able to handle this and would not react in like terms. But a teacher who is under particular strain one day, perhaps because of something that has happened elsewhere, may well come down to the child's level and react with equal emotion. This situation is not uncommon in the experience of both parents and teachers and usually it leaves the adult feeling guilty; provided, however, that the adult in question recognises what is happening, they will be prepared for their own reactions and can remain cool.

There is a theory in psychology known as Transactional Analysis or, simply, TA, which attempts to explain what is happening in communications such as the example above. The essence of the theory is that we all have what are known as three ego states. These are the Child, the Parent, and the Adult.

The Child ego state refers to the fact that we have all been children, and so there will be times when we feel as we did when a child.

The Parent ego state refers to the fact that we have all had parents or, in some cases, parent substitutes, and there will be times when we feel like our parents did.

The Adult ego state refers to the fact that as we are now adults, reality demands that we relate to others in a real or adult fashion.

Any one of these three ego states are said to predominate at any one time and they can, moreover, shift rapidly according to the situation. So there may be times when a child brings out our own child ego state and we can become like the child with the temper tantrum. It should be emphasised that the expression of our child ego state need not always be undesirable – it is not uncommon, for instance, for an adult to react with childish wonder at, say, a glorious sunset. In the case of the child with the temper tantrum, however, the teacher, more often than not, would be reminded of their own parents and so would react by expressing their parent ego state: remonstrating with the child from a position of authority. Alternatively, they may remain in their adult ego state and deal with the situation in a pragmatic fashion. The main point about TA is that it does help us to understand better what is happening in a social interchange and so helps us become better communicators.

The newcomer

'I don't go into the staffroom much. I don't think we have a lot in common.'

Most staffrooms are meant to be welcoming places and necessary havens of rest and recuperation after a busy teaching session. A school staff usually get on well together and many schools have a well-organised social programme. As in any group, however, staffrooms are made up of a number of individuals each with their own unique personalities, which sometimes can produce problems of communication, particularly for the newcomer.

The study of groups is a favourite occupation for social psychologists, who have drawn our attention to what they call 'group cohesion'. This refers to the morale of the group and the extent to which a group feels that it acts as one unit. In order for this to happen, the members of a group need to have parallel patterns of adjustment, i.e. they need to be able to share common ideals, interests, and values.

The nearer these interests are to being parallel the easier will be the level of communication. This ought not to be a problem for a group of teachers meeting in a staffroom, as presumably they all have the aims and philosophies of the school in common. These, however, are the surface patterns; the values, ideals and interests underneath are also relevant to the quality of communication. These are often known as the hidden agenda and it is this which can be a threat to a new teacher's self-esteem, as it will take time to learn this hidden agenda. For instance, there might have been discussions in the past amongst staff that have revealed a particular sensitive area, so that now, in the interests of diplomacy, this subject is never mentioned. An example of this might be where staff have discovered that there are vast differences between them in political views that in the past led to vehement disagreements. Obviously, the newcomer would not be aware of this and might easily introduce the topic in conversation only to be met with some degree of suspicion. It is all too easy for newcomers in any group to 'put their foot in it', unless they are diplomatic.

It is not unusual for the newcomer in a group to feel isolated at first and not to know why. This could be for a number of reasons: the newcomer could have more teaching qualifications than the others and some of them may feel inadequate in comparison. Or it could be simply because the other members of the group are threatened by the newcomer, whom they may see as somebody who might disrupt their group.

These days it is not uncommon to find an 'exchange teacher' on the staff of a school. Teachers from Australia and the UK regularly exchange jobs for a set period, usually one year, to their mutual benefit. There is always a period of adjustment for the newcomer which is based on cultural differences. Having worked in the UK and in Australia, I am always intrigued by the differences in social communication between the two countries. Generalisations are always dangerous but it seems to be the case that on the whole the English are more reserved than the Australians; the newcomer in England is more likely to be met by a group who may simply be expressing the common phenomenon of not being able to relate intimately with somebody until they get to know them better, which takes time. With the tradition of 'mateship' in Australia, the newcomer is much more likely to be able to fit in immediately. There are several other cultural factors which will need to be learned on an exchange. For instance, it is usual in a school or college of education in Australia for a teacher or lecturer to leave their door open when in the room; if the door is closed, that is usually a sign that the teacher or lecturer is out, but the reverse procedure seems to be the case in England.

Some patterns of behaviour are universal and it seems to be a natural phenomenon for groups which meet regularly eventually to establish their own mores and standards. Unless the newcomer is aware of this, they are liable to interpret any group's behaviour as hostile and so get off on the wrong footing and eventually may begin to feel inadequate. This could cause a newcomer to react either with aggression or with withdrawn behaviour and in so doing make communication even more difficult. It is important therefore that newcomers are not immediately judgemental of the group and that they contribute to group communication themselves by relaxing and recognising that it takes time to be accepted fully into any established group.

There are always risks of clashes of personality in any group and the discussion in Chapter 1 on basic personality differences is relevant here. However, there is usually the chance of meeting a like personality, particularly in a large staffroom.

Job satisfaction

'We only ever see the Head when there is something to complain about.'

This is a bitter statement and I would be surprised if it were found to be true in the majority of schools. However, the unpleasant fact is that in a recent survey commissioned by the Association of Teachers & Lecturers in the UK, teachers in primary schools were more dissatisfied with their heads than were workers in any of the other jobs and professions surveyed. This was a survey which included 1,878 teachers in England and Wales as well as workers in the civil service, the retail industry, and in the police. Only 51 per cent of teachers felt that their heads gave them satisfactory feedback when they had done a good job.

There are probably reasons for this state of affairs which are not always in the heads' control, and which are probably related to the increase in the heads' workload as referred to earlier. The sad fact remains, however, that job satisfaction in teaching is falling far short of what should be expected, and many teachers are feeling that their school administration is letting them down. All the research into factors affecting teacher satisfaction highlight the need they have for personal recognition. This is not surprising; as outlined in the Introduction, the need for recognition is part of our need for self-esteem and is common to us all in our kind of society. That is why the role played by the administration and particularly by the head of the school is of paramount importance in ensuring that teachers are valued for the difficult work they do. Ensuring that salaries are appropriate to their level of teaching obviously plays a part in this process but the head of the school also has a responsibility for ensuring that the staff are given regular feedback on their performance. This needs to be given routinely and not only when things go wrong.

With all the courses on management available these days, the expectation is that schools ought to be better managed, but there have been instances where this has not been so, with the result teachers are overworked and under-appreciated. One of the roles of administration in any organisation is to ensure that their staff are not overworked and that their working conditions are conducive to optimum output. Unfortunately, education has been the subject of so many cutbacks over the last two decades, both in England and in Australia, that many schools have limited resources, with teachers having to work in far from ideal conditions. Morale can soon be lowered unless this is recognised in those schools by the administration and teachers given full support for working in difficult conditions. If this is not given due recognition, morale suffers and teachers are at risk of developing stress symptoms accompanied by a lowering of self-esteem.

In the UK there are plans to introduce formal qualifications for heads of schools which will go some way to ensuring better management. The government has proposed a college for head-teachers, but unfortunately this will not become operational until the millennium. It is also unfortunate that these innovations were not introduced before the many government changes which have added to heads' changing roles and increased work-load. As things stand, many heads and teachers continue to experience reduced job satisfaction with an increasing risk of lowered self-esteem.

Job prospects and possibilities of promotion are also potential areas for reducing self-esteem. All people in employment need to feel that they have been given responsibilities commensurate with their levels of ability and qualifications. Without the possibilities for advancement or as a result of having to do work below their level of ability, teachers can soon lose heart and feel undervalued. Having to work under such circumstances for any length of time will inevitably result in a lowering of self-esteem.

School inspections

'I haven't slept properly for a week. Our school is being inspected tomorrow.'

It is right that schools should be accountable for their performances and they have usually had a positive attitude towards regular inspections both at a local level and from central office.

Until recently, inspections were generally welcomed as a time when new ideas could be introduced and advice given and readily received on improving teaching methods. Advisors (as they were called) made constructive suggestions to the school and then left knowing that their suggestions would be carried out to the general benefit of all concerned.

The situation today, however, is far removed from this constructive atmosphere and it is probably true to say that the present system of government inspections is a real threat to teachers' self-esteem and a considerable source of stress for many teachers. Stories abound of how inspectors from the Office for

Standards In Education (Ofsted) have demoralised teachers and even led to requests from heads of some schools for early retirement. It often seems that the main aim of these inspections is to 'weed out' weak teachers rather than to help schools to make necessary improvements. There are countless incidents reported of schools spending hours before an inspection preparing information for the inspectors only to be given little or no feedback afterwards. Moreover, the criteria for determining a 'good teacher' seem far from objective.

Where a teacher is already at risk of developing low self-esteem an Ofsted inspection can be the straw that breaks the camel's back. Until this system is improved it is essential that teachers accept that they are going to need some considerable support both before and after an inspection. Some support could come from colleagues who themselves have been through an inspection, but also teachers should learn how to become their own 'counsellors' as advocated in this book.

Concern for children's welfare

'I always leave the door open when I interview a child. I don't want to be accused of anything.'

It is ironical that a profession such as teaching, the very existence of which resulted from concerns for children, should be worried over possible accusations like the one above. It is a sad fact, however, that the phenomenon of child abuse in all its forms receives a great deal of attention in society these days. Research surveys indicate that there are today vastly greater numbers of cases of child abuse being reported than ever before (Jenks, 1996). Child abuse itself is not new and the reasons for its emergence as a contemporary phenomenon are open to conjecture. The fact remains, however, that there is an awareness and concern in today's society of possible child abuse that has direct implications for the teacher. Social attitudes towards children in general have changed considerably this century. In this postmodern world, children are not only cared for more than ever before but they also have legal rights (Children Act 1989). Without doubt this move has been in the best interests of children, but it has placed increased pressures upon those who look after children, including teachers.

It is not only that teachers have to see that they protect them-selves from being falsely accused of themselves abusing children. They also have to be aware of the signs of possible abuse of children by others, and ensure that if this is suspected they report it to the appropriate authorities. In today's changed political cli-mate, teachers have to concern themselves, more than ever before, with the physical, moral and emotional welfare of children. No longer are teachers merely there to educate children. It is no won-der that for some people this changing role of the teacher is a deterrent to entering the profession in the first place.

Teacher education courses are gradually recognising the need for teachers to be able to recognise the signs of child abuse and often have units on its incidence and prevalence. However, this has yet to be mandatory for all colleges, and it is sad to relate that a unit on identifying signs of child abuse was deleted from one teacher education course in Australia on the grounds of there being more pressing concerns than that one.

Some authorities are responsible for admirable innovations in this area. For instance, several in the UK have organised in-service training for teachers on identifying signs of child abuse. There is still a long way to go, however, judging from a recent survey conducted in both Australia and in the UK (Lawrence, 1998) which revealed the need for joint training in dealing with child abuse for teachers, social workers, and medical personnel.

It can be appreciated how this new focus on the child's wel-fare has resulted in a widening of the teacher's role with the added risk of job overload.

Out of school problems

'I am finding it hard to concentrate on my work these days with so much stress at home.'

That kind of comment has probably been made in many a workplace, not just in teaching. Although some people are able to forget their home problems when they are at work the evi-dence is that they cannot do so indefinitely. Eventually their whole life is affected. The teacher is notorious for 'soldiering on' in the face of other problems outside school. Teachers them-selves know only too well that they are just like other people – human beings with all the frailties of the species. They are just as likely as the rest of the population to suffer from family problems, have financial worries, and concerns about their health. Like most of us, teachers just get on with the job and try to forget outside problems when at work. Sometimes, however, these problems are so great that they are not easily left behind and they bring them into the classroom. If problems remain unresolved for long they make themselves felt in other ways, and teachers bringing problems to work can find themselves preoccupied at the least and even downright hostile to children.

Unresolved difficulties at home can soon set up a cycle of stress with feelings of guilt and inadequacy; low self-esteem is the end product of this. Very soon it affects the children's behaviour causing even lower self-esteem in the teacher. It behoves teachers therefore to ensure that they deal properly with any problems they may have outside school and not to try to ignore them. It is a mistake to think that personal problems will disappear if we stop thinking about them. The brain is like a computer in the sense that all our experiences are recorded and nothing is forgotten. Stress is cumulative and unresolved problems do not just fade away. This is evident from all the surveys into teacher stress, which is discussed further in the section on stress in Chapter 6.

Summary

The main threats to teacher self-esteem were discussed in this chapter. These range from possible feelings of inadequacy stemming from encounters with difficult parents, school inspections, lack of feedback from the head leading to poor job satisfaction, doubts about having chosen teaching as a career, coping with difficult children, and the potential difficulties faced by the new teacher. The difficulties associated with having to cope with problems outside school were also highlighted as a source of possible loss of self-esteem. The need to be aware of these threats to self-esteem before beginning a self-esteem enhancement programme was emphasised.

Revision questions

1. What are the main areas in teaching that put teachers at risk of developing low self-esteem?

2. How might the experienced teacher be at risk of developing low self-esteem?
3. What could be done to reduce the risk of low self-esteem in teaching?

Activity

Make a list of events that occurred during the last week which could have put you at risk of developing low self-esteem.

Further reading

Berne, E. (1967) *Games People Play* London: Andre Deutsch.
Harris, T. A. (1979) *I'm O.K. – You're O.K.* London: Pan Books.

Chapter 3

Characteristics of high self-esteem teachers

'*That teacher is so well organised and so popular with the children.*'

We have all come across the teacher who seems to be really on top of the job, the sort who appears to be totally relaxed and untroubled by the usual strains and stresses of teaching. The personal qualities that make up this type of teacher have been the subject of research from time to time (Burns, 1982) so that now we can identify the qualities precisely. An interesting discovery is that the personal qualities identified in effective teachers –

- a willingness to be flexible
- empathetic ability
- ability to personalise teaching
- cheerful and optimistic
- emotionally mature –

are the same as those which other research has shown to be the qualities of personality that are found also in the high self-esteem teacher. Let us consider them in turn.

A willingness to be flexible

Rigidity of thinking is one of those characteristics usually associated with low intelligence. Rigidity of personality, however, is a different matter, although it can be mistaken for low intelligence. It means not being able to change your mind when necessary, even though it may be appropriate to do so. Changing your mind in the face of new evidence is usually a sign of maturity and of a willingness to be flexible. It is certainly not always a sign of weakness. However, there are those people who seem to take a pride in never changing their minds, and it is interesting that there are some clinical studies that show that this type of person often is tense and irritable.

The teacher who is prepared to be flexible usually has high self-esteem and does not become tense and irritable when having to change the lesson timetable for instance. The teacher who is willing to be flexible would have fewer problems adjusting their teaching when a pupil suddenly becomes difficult in the classroom. If it is necessary for certain sanctions to be applied, the flexible teacher will not simply impose them rigidly without giving due consideration to the particular circumstances of the case. In short, the flexible teacher is able to be a more pragmatic teacher.

Empathetic ability

Carl Rogers (1967) has shown in counselling studies how people who are best at making positive relationships are usually those who more easily empathise with people. This means being able to feel what the other person is feeling and to communicate that feeling. It implies an ability to listen to feelings which goes beyond listening to the words in a conversation. Empathy can have a powerful effect in any relationship.

Where teachers are capable of this, it is as if a bridge has been built between the teacher and the child. The child knows that the teacher understands him or her and so feels more able to trust the teacher. The teacher who is capable of empathy eventually gets a reputation for being a good listener. This applies also to colleagues in the staffroom. Others feel they can talk to this person as there is little doubt that people feel considerable support when confiding in a person who empathises with them.

Compare the two scenes below illustrating first the absence of empathy and secondly where empathy is present.

Scene 1: Without empathy
Scene: Colleague A approaches B in the staffroom, looking distressed.

A I just have to talk to somebody about this or I'll go mad. Do you have a minute?

B OK, hang on while I put these books away, but I do have another class in 5 minutes.

A Sorry to bother you, but I do need advice from somebody on a delicate problem.

B Go ahead. What's the problem? So many people these days seem to have problems.

A I've just had this letter from the bank. I'm overdrawn on my account and I've been requested not to sign any more cheques, and the month has only just started. I don't know how I'm going to manage. [visibly distressed]

B Oh! Is that all? I thought it was going to be something really serious. It's only money.

A Well, yes, but you don't understand. I have so many bills to pay I don't know what I'm going to do.

B I can lend you a couple of quid until the end of the month if it will help.

A A couple of quid wouldn't help. I'm overdrawn to the tune of £1,000!

B Why don't you apply for a personal loan then? You're not the first one who's owed money. I think you've got this thing out of proportion, don't you?

A [bursts into tears] I feel so stupid. I can't get a loan. I've tried.

B Well, one thing I've learned and that is that crying never helps. Come on, dry your eyes. I'll be finished in half an hour and I'll take you to the pub for a drink. That'll put you right, I'm sure.

A I can't sleep at nights for worrying about it all. I just don't know what I'll do.

B Stop worrying. I've told you what to do. You could probably get a loan somewhere else you know.

A Thanks, but I don't think I could face the pub right now.

B Please yourself, but you did ask for my help.

Scene 2: With empathy
Scene: Colleague A approaches colleague B in the staffroom, looking distressed.

A I just have to talk to somebody about this or I'll go mad. Do you have a minute?

B You sound upset. Of course I have a minute. Anyway, I'm not teaching until five past ten.

A You're right. I am upset. I've just had this letter from the bank saying I have to stop signing cheques as I am well overdrawn on my account.

B That must have been a shock. It hit you pretty hard, eh? Tell me about it.

A I have so many bills to pay and no money. My son's birthday is this week and I can't even buy him a present. They might be going to cut off the electricity as I haven't been able to pay that bill for ages. And the phone as well. I can't think straight anymore, let alone teach.

B It's not easy to think straight when you get so upset, but let's have a cup of tea and try to sort this out.

A It's good of you to listen like this, but I had to tell somebody. I feel so silly.

B It does hit your self-esteem. I remember when I missed a payment on the TV and received a nasty letter as if I was criminal. Let's think about this. Have you thought of going elsewhere for a loan, another bank for instance?

A It sounds a good idea but I'm not sure they would help as my credit isn't good, is it?

B Well, it's worth a try. How about if we talk some more over at the pub when we've finished work?

A Yes, I'd like that and thanks for listening. I think I've calmed down a bit now.

B That's OK. I know you would do the same for me.

Ability to personalise teaching

Teaching is fundamentally a process of human interaction. Without denying the value of the computer and other classroom hardware, it is still the teacher as a person who is the most effective. Burns (1982) noted how in one piece of research, teachers who were described by their pupils as 'aloof and over-bearing' and did not interact with their pupils affected pupil achievements negatively. The point here is that teachers who are aloof in this way are generally afraid to 'be themselves' and have low self-esteem.

Carl Jung wrote many years ago that we all wear a persona, or mask, to some degree as a defence against the many threats to self-esteem experienced in most people's lives. However, in teaching, or in any other well-defined profession for that matter, there is always the danger of wearing the persona too rigidly and becoming a stereotype – in this case, a typical teacher. If the persona is worn too rigidly and never discarded the teacher is always the teacher, even at home in the family for instance, and the person becomes cut off from their instincts.

This state of affairs is of concern on two counts. Taken to extreme, it can result in a mental breakdown; counselling case studies have shown how some people have mental breakdowns for no other reason than that they have not been able to be themselves. The other reason why it is harmful to become a stereotype is that other people never meet the real person and so as a consequence they never really trust that person. Teachers who becomes stereotyped in this way are unable to personalise their teaching and so children do not trust them. High self-esteem teachers on the other hand are emotionally spontaneous and have an air of genuineness about them so other people are more likely to trust them.

Cheerful and optimistic

Young children tend to identify with the adults who come into regular contact with them. This is one reason why teachers have a responsibility for the child's developing personality. They easily identify with the mood of the teacher and so the teacher who is generally optimistic and cheerful usually has a happy class of children. This kind of teacher is secure in their own identity, i.e. has high self-esteem. They do not easily become upset in the face of either problems posed by the children or criticism from outside.

All children show difficult behaviour at times and it can sometimes take a supreme effort of will not to react angrily to children showing this sort of behaviour. When faced with difficulties in children, the optimistic teacher will have a belief in the child's potential for change even though at the time the child may be showing behaviour which is not easy to tolerate. The teacher who is optimistic will be able to separate the child from the behaviour and focus on the problem situation rather than seeing a problem child. In so doing they will remain in charge and not simply react to the child's misbehaviour as often happens in the not so optimistic teacher. In the latter case, the teacher is identifying with the child rather than the converse. It is a sad sight to behold a child and an adult both screaming at one another. Fortunately, this scene is rare in teaching but not uncommon between parents and children. The high self-esteem teacher has no trouble in remaining an adult under such circumstances.

Emotionally mature

Emotional maturity is difficult to define. It is a topic which has occupied the minds of philosophers throughout history and also, in latter years, the minds of psychologists. Many have tried to list qualities of personality, which they have considered to be the mark of the mature personality, but these have been no help in practice as they all seemed to add up to an impossibly ideal human being who does not exist.

Even so, many research workers have tried to define the ideal personality and then to assess emotional maturity in terms of how far a person is able to approximate to the ideal. After all, most of us have some idea of the kind of person we would call 'mature'. Even here, however, there are still problems, as different ideal qualities are defined according to circumstances. For instance, mental toughness and an ability to become insensitive to suffering would be among the ideal qualities listed when defining an emotionally mature front-line soldier. However, they would be far from the qualities listed in an emotionally mature teacher. One of the best definitions of emotional maturity which could be the basis for a suitable definition of the emotionally mature teacher comes from Gordon Allport (1938). He lists the following:

- *a sense of humour* – not just an ability to laugh at jokes but an ability to laugh at oneself. It means an absence of pomposity. It implies a sense of perspective, so that people are able to see themselves objectively, appreciating the frailties in all of us. Surveys show that children like best the teacher who has a sense of humour;
- *an ability to extend the personality* – an ability to find value and satisfaction in caring for people and other things beyond caring for oneself. It is close to a definition of altruism. Most

teachers have this quality to some degree. It is the most likely
reason for entering the profession.

- *the possessing of a unifying philosophy* – this does not necessary
imply a religious philosophy but, in the case of the teacher, it
could mean a philosophy of what education is all about – a
philosophy that it is about helping children develop their personalities and learn how to become responsible citizens as
well as teaching the basic skills of literacy and maths. In more
practical terms, it is often seen in a school's 'Mission Statement', listing the general aims and objectives of the school.
Whatever the philosophy adopted, it is manifested as consistent behaviour and consistent values; not something that is
always changing according to the situation.

The work of Erikson (1959) is also of help in defining teacher
maturity. Erikson views life as a series of eight stages through
which we have to pass successfully in order to achieve maturity.
The teacher should have successfully gone through the various
stages of childhood and adolescence ready to become creative and
self-fulfilling in their chosen profession. They will be ready to take
on new opportunities in life with zest and with a strong sense of
their own identity. If, on the other hand, they have not been able to
pass successfully through any of the previous stages, they would
show guilt and self-doubt with corresponding low self-esteem.

However we define emotional maturity, it is clear that the
high self-esteem teacher is also usually the one considered to be
emotionally mature. The high self-esteem teacher will be generally optimistic and cheerful, and they will be secure in their own
identity. As already discussed, this is the second aspect of our
definition of self-esteem in practice. All children at some stage of
their lives are difficult and will test the teacher's patience. The
emotionally mature teacher with high self-esteem will not easily
become upset by difficult behaviour in children or by criticism
from others.

Summary

The main qualities of personality that contribute to high self-
esteem in the teacher were discussed in this chapter. The
important quality of empathy was particularly emphasised.

Those personal qualities that combine to make a mature person were also discussed.

Revision questions

1. What are the five main characteristics of the high self-esteem teacher?
2. What is meant by 'empathy'?
3. How can teachers develop the quality of empathy?

Activity

Seek the cooperation of a colleague. A tells B of an emotional event in their life, a holiday, a house move, a change of job. A talks about it for 5 minutes while B 'listens actively' to the feelings behind the words, commenting after each sentence on the emotion being communicated by A, e.g. 'That sounds as if you were happy.' The roles are then reversed and the procedure is repeated.

Further reading

Branden, N. (1995) *Six Pillars of Self-esteem*. London: Bantam.

Burns, R. (1982) *Self-Concept Development in Education*. Sydney: Holt, Rinehart and Winston.

Rogers, C. R. (1967) *On Becoming A Person*. London: Constable.

Chapter 4

Improving communication skills

'I never seem to be able to get my point across at staff meetings.'

If asked, most teachers would say that they are good communicators; after all they have had to learn to direct a class, give instructions and ask questions. They may well add, 'Isn't that a major part of my job?' Of course, communication is an important aspect of a teacher's job, but some teachers do not find it easy, especially in formal meetings. It is not that they are shy but rather for some reason, such as nervousness or lack of confidence, they tend to become either aggressive or too submissive to be taken seriously. The aim should be to use assertive behaviour and this is defined in a precise way.

Assertive behaviour

There are different styles of communication, and some are more effective than others. The recommended style is the one known as *assertive behaviour*. This means being able to make statements clearly, precisely, and confidently. People with low self-esteem have a problem with this method of communication, and as a result they generally communicate in one of two opposite ways, depending on their innate temperament.

If they are of an extraverted temperament they tend to use a bombastic, loud-voiced approach, attempting to ride roughshod over others. This is the 'little man with the big voice' syndrome, desperately trying to compensate for underlying feelings of inadequacy. The more introverted temperament will attempt to communicate through passive, compliant behaviour – the 'little mouse' syndrome.

Both these styles of communication produce tensions in others, so inhibiting good communication. People at these extremes certainly communicate, but in a negative way; they communicate a lack of trust and they also usually give a false impression of their true selves. On the other hand, the person using the assertive method of communication is neither aggressive nor passive but is able to communicate clearly and openly without anxiety and in a confident manner. Assertive behaviour lies in the middle of a continuum of types of communication. Imagine drawing a line. At one end there is *submissive* behaviour and at the other end there is *aggressive* behaviour. *Assertive* behaviour is in the middle, as the diagram shows.

Submissive	Assertive	Aggressive
vague statements	*objective statements*	*punitive statements*
'Now look what you've done'	'You have made a mess'	'I'll get you for that!'
'I'm sorry to bother you but . . .'	'I need a ride to school'	'Give me a ride!'

Using the assertive method of communication depends not only on employing the correct phrases but also in ensuring that these are synchronised with the correct body language or non-verbal communication. The typical *submissive* statement is generally made with the head down, eyes looking at the floor, and in a weak voice. The typical *aggressive* statement is made with head forward, eyes narrowed, and loudly in a harsh voice. The typical *assertive* statement is generally made with head held high, eye contact maintained throughout, voice strong and modulated.

It is vital to consider non-verbal communication in any self-esteem enhancement programme.

Non-verbal communication

Research shows that communication consists of more than verbal utterances. The work of Michael Argyle (1997) shows us clearly that non-verbal behaviour in itself is also a powerful means of communication: people do not always need words to communicate.

The area of non-verbal communication has received a lot of attention from research workers over the years. Mannerisms, facial expressions, body posture, eye contact and tone of voice can all express meaning in different ways according to how a person is feeling at the time. Often this non-verbal communication is more powerful than what is actually said. For instance, there is some evidence to show that people will remember the contents of a lecture, given up to 12 months previously, far less well than what the lecturer was wearing and what the lecturer sounded like. Recalling our school days, most of us will remember what our teachers sounded like, looked like and whether we liked them or not, even though we do not easily recall what they actually said to us.

Some research has shown that a class of children will soon learn whether their teacher likes them, cares about their output, or feels they are inferior creatures, without a word being spoken to them. Moreover, it seems that non-verbal behaviour is usually transmitted unconsciously in contrast to verbal messages which can be manipulated more easily. There are always individual differences in this respect. Some people, for instance, find it much easier than others to tell lies. Whereas one person may be able to tell a lie without batting an eyelid, the next person may not be able to do so without going red in the face and stammering.

A teacher with low self-esteem may feel anxious or nervous in front of a class but try hard to say positive things in an attempt to hide their feelings. The bad news from the research into non-verbal behaviour shows that they cannot completely hide their true feelings in this way indefinitely – their non-verbal behaviour will give the game away. Non-verbal messages are transmitted through voice tone, extent of eye contact, hand gestures, facial expressions and body posture, and children are not easily fooled. In fact, there is some evidence to show that children are more sensitive to these non-verbal cues than adults. Without a word being spoken they can tell if the teacher likes them or cares about their work.

So what can teachers do to improve their communication skills? Firstly, they need to ensure that they are correctly using assertive behaviour, and, secondly, they need to ensure that their verbal and non-verbal messages are synchronised.

Using the right words

For some people even knowing what words to use is a problem, let alone having to learn how to synchronise them with their body language. They hate formal meetings where they may be called upon to speak and often dry up when the time comes. They are always afraid that they will make fools of themselves and so become over-anxious; as they experience fear, anxiety interferes with their thinking. The simple remedy for this problem is to be prepared beforehand and to practise the words to be used. If it is known that a forthcoming meeting is going to be a stressful experience then the first few sentences at least should be rehearsed. Having rehearsed in advance precisely what to say, the situation is a little less fearsome and with continued practice such people gradually come to fear meetings less.

Whilst it is a simple matter to rehearse for meetings in this way, using the right words in a conflict situation requires more preparation. It is all too easy to become too emotional in such a situation, but it is still important to try to stick to the assertive formula when composing your assertive statement. This is the **I–when–because** formula:

- The assertive statement should begin with the word **I** followed by your feeling about the situation, e.g. 'I feel upset . . .' or 'I feel embarrassed . . .' or 'I feel unhappy . . .', etc.
- This should be followed by the word **when**, e.g. 'when that happens . . .' or 'when I am asked to do too many things . . .' or 'when you say things like that . . .' etc.
- This should be followed by the word **because**, e.g. 'because I cannot do my work' or 'because I need more time' or 'because I cannot think properly'.

Using this formula may seem artificial at first but it becomes easier to use with practice. Main points to note are:

- Preparation is the key to assertive communication – forewarned is to be forearmed.
- By using 'I' you are demonstrating strength in being able to express your feelings.
- By using 'when' you are showing that the problem is not forevermore but only 'when' those particular circumstances apply.

- By using 'because' you are showing that your point is not merely a capricious whim but rather you have a logical reason for it.
- The order of the formula – I, when, because – can be varied according to the situation.

Developing assertive behaviour

'I feel annoyed when I am asked to do extra duties without warning because it gives me very little time to prepare.'

Starting a conversation with an assertive statement is only the beginning of being assertive. It is necessary next to be able to use reflective listening and the broken record technique. These should be used in the following sequence:

1. Listen: sit quietly and wait for the respondent to reply.
2. Listen reflectively: this means empathising with (not patronising) the respondent and showing that you understand their right to have a different point of view, e.g. 'I understand how you feel about this and I can see your point.'
3. The broken record: this means restating your position, still using the 'I–when–because' formula, and possibly expanding on it, e.g. 'Even so, I have to tell you I am unhappy about having to work during my free time as I do need the extra time for my other work.'

In a real-life situation, of course, such a dialogue would have many more exchanges than this, but the formula can provide the basis of the interchanges. This procedure may not totally resolve a conflict but at least you will have asserted yourself and have maintained your self-esteem.

Now consider the following scene between a teacher and a parent:

Scene: A parent has made an appointment to see you and is complaining to you that their child is not being treated fairly. They say you have told him that he has to raise his hand when he wants to speak to you in the middle of a lesson and are always picking on him. You are trying to help this child learn how to control his impulsive behaviour which has been disrupting the whole class. You have rehearsed your words prior to the parent's visit.

Teacher [after preliminary greetings] I feel disappointed to have to tell you that when your child shouts out in class nobody here can get on with their work.

Parent You have been victimising my child and I am not putting up with it.

Teacher I am sorry you feel angry. Clearly you think I have been picking on your child. I am disappointed to have to tell you all this and that I am not able to continue the lesson because of the disruptive behaviour. My aim is to try to help him control the behaviour.

Parent What! I have never heard such nonsense! You are not trying to help him, you are trying to destroy him and I've had enough of it!

Teacher I can see that you are still upset about all this. How do you think we should have dealt with the situation?

Parent You should have just ignored it. He's not that bad.

Teacher I was not victimising him. I was merely trying to help him control his disruptive behaviour because I cannot get on with the lesson with all that interruption.

Parent I still think you are victimising him. You should have ignored him.

Teacher If I had ignored him, then the others would have thought that the behaviour was OK and they would have done the same. When disruptive behaviour is ignored, other children usually copy and eventually there is chaos and nothing learned.

Parent I have never heard such stupid nonsense. My child is never that bad.

Teacher I can see that you are not happy with this, but what do you think I should have done if the whole class had started to shout out aloud in the middle of the lesson?

Parent I don't know. That's for you to deal with not me.

Teacher Would you like to sit in the class at some stage to watch what is going on?

Parent I think that's a good idea.

Teacher Right, let's fix a time.

Parent I can be free any morning.

Teacher How about tomorrow at 10 o'clock?

Parent   Good! See you tomorrow then.
Teacher Goodbye, and thanks for coming.

Again, in real life that scene may not have been altogether accurate, as many other things would probably have been said. However, it does illustrate:

- the need to have rehearsed the appropriate words to use so that the teacher is not caught unawares;
- the need to empathise with the parent and let them have their say even if the teacher does not agree with it;
- the 'I–when–because' formula used in a more flexible fashion;
- the use of the 'broken record' technique.

Note that the teacher referred to a 'problem situation' and not to a 'problem child'; this helped diffuse the parent's anger.

Being genuine

The use of assertive behaviour depends not only on being able to use the right words as described but also on the ability to be what Carl Rogers has described as 'genuine'. People who are genuine are those who are able to 'be themselves' and have the courage to say exactly what they feel without fear. Needless to say, these people usually have high self-esteem. The good news again is that 'genuineness' comes as self-esteem rises, although it can be learned consciously through practice. But it is not something that comes easily to many people in our kind of culture.

The Anglo-Saxon races, for instance, are renowned for being more reserved than their Latin neighbours. We all have a certain degree of reserve. It could be argued that in the interests of smooth social intercourse it would not do to go around always revealing our true thoughts, especially if we know it will cause hurt to others. However, some people wear what Carl Jung has called the 'persona' or mask to such an extent that nobody ever knows who they really are. Consequently, they are not easily trusted. It is important therefore that we develop genuineness in ourselves in the interests of good communication as well as better mental health.

Good communication checklist

The following good communication checklist should be completed by teachers wishing to check that their communication skills are satisfactory. The list has been compiled from areas which the research evidence has shown to be important in the classroom.

Verbal behaviour
- Do you always address children politely?
- Do you use their first names when talking to them?
- Do you use words they understand?'
- Do you always give clear instructions?

Non-verbal behaviour
- Do you always use eye contact?
- Do you smile a lot?
- Does your voice sound friendly?
- Do you use mannerisms?

Establishing trust
- Do you express your own feelings easily?
- Do your pupils know the kind of person you are?
- Do your pupils know that you care about them?
- Do you give pupils responsible tasks to do?

Presenting a positive model
- Are you generally a confident and cheerful person?
- Are you always fair when dealing with difficult behaviour?
- Do you look for things in your pupils to praise?
- Do children always know what you expect from them?

Developing expectancies
- Do you demonstrate confidence in pupils' abilities to learn?
- Do you communicate that you expect appropriate behaviour?
- Are you optimistic regarding pupils' abilities to change?
- Do you use positive commands rather than negative ones?

Assertive behaviour checklist

Use the following checklist to assess whether you are using assertive behaviour in your communications:

- Forgive yourself your past mistakes.
- Learn to take responsibility for your own feelings.
- Learn how to use the 'I–when–because' formula.
- Recognise that it is all right to make mistakes, provided you learn from them.
- Express pleasure at your successes and share them with others.
- Accept that it is all right to change your mind, as sometimes circumstances change.
- Do not be pressurised into making decisions where you may need time to think.
- Learn to ask for what you want rather than waiting for others to notice.
- Make plans for each day as well as for the future.
- Respect other people's rights also to be assertive.

Summary

This chapter focused on helping teachers understand the need for effective communication. The use of *assertive* behaviour was illustrated and contrasted with *aggressive* and *submissive* behaviour. Examples were used to show that assertive behaviour depends not only on the correct words but also on being able to synchronise these with appropriate body language.

Revision questions

1. What is the difference between aggressive and assertive behaviour?
2. Why is non-verbal behaviour an important aspect of communication?
3. What is the 'I–when–because' formula?

Activity

Complete the following table under the appropriate heading using the 'I–when–because' formula. The first one has been done as an illustration:

Scene	Feeling	Behaviour	Effect
Colleague regularly uses your pen without asking.	I feel angry . . .	when you keep borrowing my pen without permission . . .	as I have to search for another one.
1. Colleague always interrupts you immediately after you have started a new lesson.			
2. Colleagues regularly keep you waiting in your car although you have offered them a lift home.			
3. The caretaker keeps leaving a mess on the floor in your classroom after emptying the wastepaper basket.			

Further reading

Argyle, M. (1997) *Psychology of Interpersonal Behaviour*. Harmondsworth: Penguin.

Gordon, T. (1974) *Teacher Effectiveness Training*. New York: Wyden.

Wilson, B. (1996) *The Assertive Teacher*. Aldershot: Arena.

Chapter 5

Locus of control

'I never plan much as things never seem to work out as I expect them to.'

We have all met the kind of person with a tendency to be pessimistic about life and who seems always to look on the dark side. Then again, there is the opposite personality, those successful people who seem to be in charge of their lives and tend to 'make things happen'. The former tend to be the followers in life while the latter tend to be the leaders, although, like most human traits which are measured by psychologists, people are really a little of each depending upon the circumstances. This concept of human behaviour has occupied the minds of research workers for the last few decades and is known as locus of control.

Being in control

Locus of control is a phrase which is rarely encountered in teaching, despite the fact that it has been shown to be of profound significance in any programme aimed at increasing morale. It is a learned phenomenon, referring to the extent to which people feel that they are in control of their lives, and can be measured along a continuum.

At one end of the continuum are those who believe that they have little control over their lives. These people are known as externally controlled, and they feel that all the misfortunes in their lives are the result of external forces outside their control. As a result they tend to be apathetic and accepting of their lot. If, on the other hand, they are successful, they tend to believe that they were simply lucky and their personality, or self, played no real part in their luck.

Those people at the other end of the continuum are known as internally controlled, and they believe the opposite – that their fate is very much in their own hands. They believe that their successes and failures are the result of their own behaviour. As a result, these people tend to be more striving and achievement-orientated, always trying to improve their lot. When they succeed, they regard their success as justification of their efforts. On the other hand, if they fail, they blame themselves, even though there may be evidence that the failure was not their fault.

Clearly, both extreme attitudes are unrealistic and can lead to problems of personality adjustment. Fortunately, although these extremes do exist, in practice most people seem to exhibit a little of each trait.

Research into the locus of control has gradually gained momentum over the last few years and the concept is now recognised, along with that of self-esteem, as of extreme importance in personality improvement programmes. The main reason for this is that there seems to be a positive correlation between self-esteem and locus of control. People who are of high self-esteem are usually more internally controlled. Moreover, there is some evidence to show that there is a causal relationship at work, so that people whose experiences in life have taught them to be more externally controlled gradually develop low self-esteem. This research has profound consequences for the morale of any industrial organisation. It implies that unless workers feel that they have a say in the running of their organisation they are in danger of becoming externally controlled, and of developing low self-esteem. Also, there is evidence that the pessimists in society tend to be the externally controlled while the optimists are the internally controlled. The implications of this research for the teaching profession and for schools are obvious.

Although schools are generally run along democratic lines, there are exceptions to this and it is incumbent on the heads of all schools to ensure that the staff are involved in decision making. This research also has implications for local and central government whose policies sometimes are imposed on schools after only the minimum of consultation. Under these circumstances, it comes as no surprise to discover, for example, that some teachers are uneasy about the newly introduced 'literacy hour' (which has now been supplemented with the 'numeracy hour'!). The fact that most primary teachers have always devoted a set time to literacy each day is bound to be a source of irritation, but the main concern and unease of teachers stems from not having been properly consulted before this was decided.

A real danger of the Ofsted system of inspections is its potential for reducing self-esteem by fostering externally controlled behaviour in teachers. After an inspection, teachers are often left feeling that they have little control over their work. Stories abound of schools being inspected and frequently receiving either negative or very little feedback. The effect of this on teachers is to leave them feeling powerless. This can produce a feeling of failure which is quite damaging for many teachers. There is recent anecdotal evidence to suggest that there are a number of schools where teachers have reported sick with stress-related illnesses immediately after an inspection.

Whenever a failure experience occurs, people generally react in one of two ways, depending largely on their locus of control. The more internally controlled will tend to react by withdrawing with strong feelings of personal inadequacy as they are more inclined to blame themselves. The more externally controlled will tend to react with a more cavalier 'don't care' attitude, refusing to bear any responsibility for the failure. In both cases, the motivation for taking action will have been reduced.

Whilst teachers, like the rest of us are, are often at the mercy of government policy, and indeed in some areas of life appear often to have very little control over their welfare, there is one area in which they can influence their locus of control. This is in the setting of personal goals.

Setting goals

By giving some thought to goal setting, people can gradually change their locus of control, and as a consequence enhance their self-esteem. The problem for the teacher is that it is all too easy to become embroiled in the immediacy of classroom teaching, often compounded by frenetic attempts to combine the demands of home and job, so that there is rarely a chance to reflect on where they are going in life. Possibly the only time that teachers are able to give thought to this is during a holiday, when there is little incentive to become too reflective! The fact is that the setting of goals in life is a major route to internal locus of control and high self-esteem. Unless people are consciously aware of their goals in life, there is always the tendency to let opportunities for advancement slip by until one day they wake up and there are no more opportunities.

The person who is able to set goals has a distinct feeling of being in charge of their life. The locus of control is firmly with the person who knows where they are going. Goals are of two kinds – long-term and short-term. The nature of the job means that teachers usually are well versed in setting short-term goals; this is evident in the planning of lessons and in the day-to-day management of the classroom. It is long-term goal setting which tends to be ignored.

An exercise in long-term goal setting

List below in order of importance three goals for the future.

1. . . . .
2. . . . .
3. . . . .

Taking each goal in turn, plan along the lines of:

My goal is to . . . .
I will achieve my goal by . . . .
Time taken to achieve it will be . . . .

Note that the planning of the goal involves three factors: being specific in stating it, being specific with regard to the means of achieving it and being specific with regard to the timespan. Using this method of specificity makes the goal more real and prevents it from being too general. For example:

My goal is to obtain a degree in Mathematics.
I will achieve my goal by doing an external course through the local college.

Time taken to achieve it will be three years from the date of registration.

Note that the goal was specific. To have stated simply that 'My goal is to have a higher degree as soon as I have the time' would have been far too general.

Summary

This chapter introduced the concept of locus of control, showing how some people appear to feel that they have very little control over their lives, in contrast with those who feel that everything that happens to them can be attributed to their efforts. It was also shown how the locus of control concept is related to self-esteem. Finally, the importance of goal setting was emphasised and suggestions made on how to go about this.

Revision questions

1. What are at the extremes of the locus of control continuum?
2. How is locus of control related to the self-esteem concept?
3. Why should setting goals change the locus of control?

Activity

Complete the questionnaire on the opposite page to assess your Locus of Control, circling the responses that best describe how you would feel in these situations.

Further reading

Hopson, B. and Scall, M. (1981) *Lifeskills Teaching*. London: McGraw Hill.
Phares, E. J. (1976) *Locus of Control in Personality*. New Jersey: General Learning Press.
Seligman, M. (1991) *Learned Optimism*. London: Random House.
Weiner, B. *et al.* (1971) *Perceiving the Causes of Success and Failure*. New Jersey: General Learning Press.

Locus of Control

1. If you were caught exceeding the speed limit while driving, would it be
   (a) because you often drive too fast

   or

   (b) just because you were unlucky?

2. When illness causes you to be absent form work, would it be more likely that
   (a) you had picked up another person's germs

   or

   (b) you were run down at the time?

3. When bored in a lecture, is it more likely because at the time
   (a) your mind was on something else

   or

   (b) the lecturer had a boring style?

4. When you can't find the classroom waste paper basket, is it more likely that
   (a) you had mislaid it

   or

   (b) the caretaker has not replaced it?

5. When you are praised for doing good work, would it be more likely that
   (a) the person praising you does not know all the facts

   or

   (b) you really did deserve the praise?

6. If a child brought you a bunch of flowers, would it be more likely that
   (a) the child was trying to curry favour with you

   or

   (b) the child genuinely wanted to show friendship?

Scoring:
Give yourself 2 points if you have circled 1a 2b 3a 4a 5b 6b.
The higher the score, the more internally controlled.

Chapter 6

How to manage stress

'I feel so tired every morning and I dread having to go into school these days.'

That kind of statement is a common expression of stress, or burn-out. It might sound a bit extreme but actually it is not as rare as it may seem. In fact, the main impetus for writing this book came from personal observation of teacher stress both in the UK and in Australia as well as from the many surveys conducted. Teachers today are more at risk of developing stress symptoms than at any other time in the history of the profession. The number of teachers on sick leave and applying for early retirement because of 'nervous strain' has steadily increased over the last couple of decades.

Of course, all jobs and professions have their share of people suffering stress for various reasons and the source of the stress may not always be the work they do. It is significant, however, that in teaching, research shows that it is the job itself which is the main source of stress. In a matched study comparing teachers with people under stress in other professions, Cox *et al.* (1978) found that 79 per cent of teachers mentioned their job as the main source of their stress whereas only 38 per cent of non-teachers cited their job. Pratt (1978) found a greater incidence of stress in the teaching profession than in any other.

Both these studies took place some time ago but there is no reason to think that the situation today is any different, judging from the 1998 survey conducted by the Opinion Research Corporation (UK). After surveying the attitudes of 45 different work organisations, they concluded that workload was a common stress factor and only 45 per cent of teachers in the survey considered themselves to be happy in their work. This compares with the earlier Pratt survey, when 60.4 per cent of teachers expressed some nervous strain, and only 51.1 per cent of people in other professions and 36.1 per cent of people in other jobs said they were under stress. This type of survey has been conducted over the years in the UK, in Australia and in the USA, and all show similar findings.

The following list of tasks presented to teachers in a state school in Western Australia in 1998 is one example of the pressure faced by teachers today. This list, which had to be completed in one term, would be instantly recognisable to most teachers in schools in the UK:

Quality assurance reports – monitoring of students' performance

Developing a policy for students at risk

Completion of a behaviour management policy (three meetings on this after school)

Developing a risk management plan

Developing a crisis management plan

School development plan

Technology 2000 (four-year plan)

Curriculum implementation plan

Data collection for critical analysis of student performance

Four staff meetings (after school)

The irony and the pity of all this is that nobody would deny the value of implementing this programme. The concern is that all these events are extra to the teacher's normal working day. Moreover, it is not the amount of work itself which can cause stress; the problem is in not having sufficient time to complete it. Workload is almost certainly a common stress factor these days as teachers are expected to do so much more and have so little time available. No longer can it be denied that teaching is a high-risk profession compared with other jobs.

The following are other sources of stress regularly cited in the surveys:

- difficult staff relationships;
- uncooperative children;

- feelings of inadequacy regarding teaching (the most regularly mentioned);
- aggressive children;
- extra duties;
- concern for childrens' learning;
- role conflict.

Apart from these broad categories taken from various surveys, other sources of stress commonly identified are:

- achievement recognition;
- limited promotion prospects;
- difficult interpersonal relationships;
- minimal input in decision making;
- difficult children;
- low status;
- inadequate salary;
- limited teaching resources;
- poor relationships with administrators.

Once we accept the fact that teaching is a high risk profession in this respect and are able to identify its sources then perhaps we can set about finding ways to prevent it.

Defining stress

Before outlining methods of coping with stress, we need to know how to recognise it. As with many concepts in psychology, the words used have a meaning outside the profession as well as within it, so it is important to define it precisely. For instance, some writers assert that a modicum of 'stress' is desirable and motivating. Their definition of stress is much wider than the one preferred here. They are probably referring to the well-known observation that before any activity can be successfully completed the person has to be in a state of readiness; this includes increased adrenaline flow and a generally raised level of excitement. This is sometimes known as the 'flight or fight' response and research does indicate that a modicum of this is healthy, although too much is not. There would appear to be an optimum level of this kind of stress required for different tasks. The inverted U-shaped curve in Figure 6.1 illustrates this. It also illustrates how a person with no anxiety, i.e. no adrenaline flow, will have no performance. Equally, the person with no points of anxiety at the other end of the axis will also have no performance. On the other hand, the person in the middle of the axis with 5 points of anxiety will have maximum performance at 10 points.

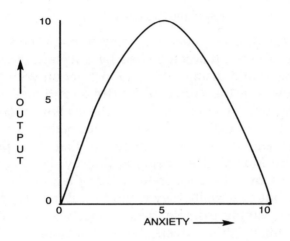

Figure 6.1

The preferred definition for our purpose is one based on the work of Hans Selye (1976) and focuses on the need to include some reference to adverse physiological reactions. Paraphrasing his definition, stress occurs when *the demands of a job are greater than our response capability, with resultant unpleasant consequences.*

Applying this definition of stress to teaching, as the demands in teaching increase a point is bound to come when stress will occur. Moreover, there are grounds for believing stress to be cumulative in its effects. The evidence is that at first people simply get on with the job and try to deny stress. With time, however, unless dealt with as they happen, stressful events pile up one on top of another until eventually the situation overwhelms.

To further complicate the picture, individual personalities react differently to the same stress factors; in other words some people break down earlier than others. However, it is important to recognise that we all have our breaking point; it's just that this point comes earlier for some than for others, depending mainly on innate temperament, combined with different life experiences.

So what happens when people experience stress? People under stress usually report both psychological reactions and bodily reactions.

Psychological reactions

The first inclination of something being wrong is best described as a feeling of tension accompanied by a feeling of irritability. Most people would dismiss this and just get on with the job in hand. If, however, the source of the stress continues or is compounded by other sources of stress, the feeling of tension increases and eventually spills over into bodily activity. For instance, an ambitious teacher discovers that their promotion prospects are limited. They begin at first by denying this, and then perhaps by trying to pretend that they do not care for promotion, but eventually they begin to feel moody, dispirited, become increasingly irritable, find themselves often criticising others, and finally show adverse bodily reactions.

Bodily reactions

Distinct and measurable bodily reactions usually accompany any kind of psychological tension. So a feeling of irritability will soon be accompanied by an increase in heart rate and blood pressure. The skeletal system will become tense and the respiration will become shallow. Adrenaline will be secreted and 'butterflies in the stomach' will be felt. These are the short-term reactions. Of more concern are the long term physiological responses.

With continued stress, all the organs of the body will be 'on alert' and put under extra strain. It can be appreciated just how prolonged extra strain on the body can eventually produce a physical breakdown. So what starts as psychologically perceived stress eventually becomes physical stress, and exhaustion sets in. This is what is usually referred to as a 'nervous breakdown'.

The specific ways in which the body reacts to stress varies with the individual, but in the initial stages, following a build-up of stress, most people will find themselves with sleep disturbances, i.e. either finding it hard to get off to sleep, or waking in the middle of the night and wondering why they can't sleep. Headaches are common and also erratic bowel movements. More serious physical symptoms can occur; amongst these are backache, weight loss, decreased resistance to infection, reduced sex drive and viral illnesses as even the immune system can become affected.

Dealing with the stress

There are many events which occur throughout the teacher's week that can become stressful unless they are tackled. In the regular hurly-burly of teaching, it is all too easy to dismiss irritating events without taking the time to handle them constructively. Unfortunately, the emotional effects of these experiences remain and if the events continue to occur the effects accumulate, so that eventually they are perceived out of all proportion to the single experiences. An example of this would be a teacher facing a child who continues to challenge the teacher despite all efforts to help. This would be accepted by most teachers as a normal aspect of the job. However, if the teacher also has to contend with an awkward meeting with a parent, and this is then followed by a difficult staff meeting and then by finding that their car has a flat tyre, the last of these things could be the final straw!

There have been several surveys over the years into how teachers cope with stress. It seems that there are three methods teachers use.

1 Denial

The first and most common method teachers use is to deny that stress exists. In fact, this is the most likely reaction when anybody first encounters stress. It works in those cases where the situation might change soon after the event. For example, if a teacher has had to take on extra duties and finds this stressful, they might just dismiss this as something they have to get on with. Then a new teacher is appointed; the source of the stress is removed before it could do damage. If on the other hand, the extra duties remain for any length of time and it becomes increasingly difficult for the teacher to cope, the stress cannot be denied indefinitely. Even if the teacher tries hard to deny it, the chances are that stress symptoms will follow simply because the brain never forgets an experience. It may not be in the conscious mind but it will certainly be in the unconscious and ready to burst into consciousness often when least expected. Moreover, as mentioned earlier, stress is cumulative and one event can pile on top of another, which means that it is just not humanly possible to continue to ignore stress indefinitely. So this method is not to be recommended.

2 Sharing

The second most common method of coping with stress is to discuss it with somebody close, usually the partner or spouse, which can help to reduce the stress. The only problem with this is that it requires somebody who can empathise with the stress and unless the partner has also been a teacher it is difficult for them fully to appreciate the emotions that the stressed teacher goes through. Even where the partner is a teacher, it is not easy for them to help as they are just as likely themselves to need to talk about their own teaching experiences. Even so, this method is probably to be preferred to trying to deny it.

3 Action

The third method and the one recommended is first to stop denying the stress but to recognise it, and then to take some kind of constructive action, i.e. to acknowledge that there are symptoms that need attention.

The kind of attention taken can be either a direct attack by removing the source of the stress, or through strategies designed to increase the capacity to cope with the stress.

Removing the source of the stress

There will be some sources of stress which can be removed by improved planning or more efficient organisation. One example of this is stress which stems from the administrative side of the teacher's workload. The principles of *time management* are often quoted as a means of dealing with this kind of stress. Teachers have so much paperwork and records to keep that the principles of time management are particularly relevant to most of them. There is nothing magical about time management and in fact much of it is a matter of using commonsense. Even so, it should not be decried, as the very act of considering time management is beneficial, involving as it does 'taking stock' of the teaching day. The following questionnaire would be an example of the kind of planning tackled by time management:

1. Do you plan and write down your goals for the whole term?
2. Do you break these goals down into jobs to be done each day?
3. Are you able to prioritise your goals?
4. Do you delegate some jobs?
5. Do you keep up-to-date records of each child's progress?
6. Do you estimate the time taken to complete each daily task?
7. Do you reassess your goals in view of the time taken?
8. Are you able to be selective regarding attendance at meetings?
9. Do you ensure you always have spares for disposable equipment?
10. Do you have time allocated for seeing children with difficulties?

No doubt there are countless other tasks involved in a teaching day which will be worth considering from the point of view of time management. The teacher should try to take time to reflect on them and so decide for themselves the areas they think can be improved. Using this approach it should be possible to identify those sources of stress emanating from the administrative work and then to decide whether it would be possible to remove them.

Many sources of stress could be removed simply by delegation. One example of this would be the keeping of attendance records. Some schools are experimenting with removing this chore through electronic methods, while some are considering delegating it to an ancillary. There are probably many such cases of non-teaching duties that could be delegated to an ancillary, leaving the teacher free to concentrate on teaching.

Increasing the capacity to cope with stress

Having gone through this exercise, it is quite likely that there will be sources of stress which cannot be removed. In these cases there are strategies that teachers can learn which are designed to increase their capacity to cope with the stress. The aim this time would be to confront the source of stress without experiencing unpleasant emotions. The strategy involves a combination of behavioural analysis techniques and creative visualisation and can be most effective if combined with the principles of rational-emotive therapy. The main attraction of this approach is that it is a self-help method and can be practised at home.

Rational-emotive therapy

Rational-emotive therapy (RET) owes its origins to Albert Ellis (1979), a New York psychologist who had become disenchanted with Freudian psychoanalysis. It is more confrontational than traditional psychotherapy and as a result it was met at first with much scepticism. However, following several research evaluations of the method, it is now considered by most therapists to be a useful and effective method of help for people showing all sorts of emotional and personality problems, ranging from ways of dealing with difficulties in personal relationships to severe depression and extreme anxiety states. It is recognised by clinicians as a more useful method of help than the more analytic methods traditionally used in psychotherapy. Traditional psychotherapy relied heavily on the role of the therapist, whereas in RET the client does most of the work and is actively involved in their own treatment.

Principles of RET
A fundamental principle of RET is that our emotions are usually caused by our thinking. For instance, we might say 'That child makes me angry' when in fact it is not *the child* who makes us angry – we make *ourselves* angry by the way we have interpreted

the situation. We interpret situations in terms of our own personalities.

Imagine two friends who have been brought up as children in two radically different environments. The first had a country childhood and lived in the Australian Outback. The second was brought up in an English city. They are both walking in an English park when suddenly a grass snake appears in their path. The first person might interpret the appearance of the snake as a joyful sight as it reminds them of their happy childhood. They would think of this and react with joy. The second person probably has never seen a snake before but has heard that they can kill and so interprets the sudden sight of a snake as a threat and is afraid. They would think about this and react with fear. The stimulus is the same for each person but it is interpreted in different ways with accompanying different emotional reactions. In each case, the different emotions are caused by their different thinking. This is one of the basic principles in RET and is the one which is most useful as a basis for stress management. This principle states that whenever a person reacts emotionally to a specific situation, the emotion felt is a direct result of their interpretation of the situation.

If we can learn to reinterpret a potentially negative stressful situation positively then positive emotions will take the place of negative ones. The key to stress management, then, is to learn how to do this and the first step is to learn how to change our thinking. It should be emphasised that a change in thinking is only the first step in the process. It is not enough just to change our thinking as in the case of the football team coach who exhorts his team to chant 'We are going to win' and then they go out and lose! Positive and permanent changes need to follow. To this end, it would be helpful to apply the principles of RET in the context of the four-stage process outlined in the next section. This is often referred to as the ABCDE approach:

A = The activating event (the source of the stress)
B = The belief held (the thinking about it)
C = The consequences of the thinking (the emotions)
D = The disputation (a rational appraisal of the situation)
E = The effect of the disputation (the rational solution)

In practice, the ABCDE approach is incorporated into four stages.

The four-stage process in reducing stress

Stage 1

Using pen and paper, analyse the stressful event under the same headings as those appearing against A, B, C, D, E above.

Activating event (A). Describe the exact circumstances: 'I am being criticised by the parents of a child I teach.'

Consequences (C). Describe how you feel: 'I feel so depressed.'

Thinking or belief (B). What went through your mind at the time? 'I am no good as a teacher.'

And so on.

Stage 2

Disputation (D). Be rational about your thinking and challenge it scientifically: 'Where is the evidence I am no good?'

It is necessary to be firm with yourself in this stage; dismiss any negative thoughts and decide to think only of the good things in your personality, e.g. you are a qualified teacher so you cannot be stupid and cannot be a bad person as your motives for being a teacher were laudable. The main point here is to think positively about yourself. It may be necessary to reflect for a few minutes on the positive things about yourself in general. Some of the following should be on your list: a good listener, a helpful person, brave, a good sense of humour, creative, understanding, kind.

After this exercise, compose sentences containing positive statements. These should also be the opposite of the negative ones listed when defining the stressful thinking, e.g. 'I cannot be a stupid person as I have a teaching qualification. I am a nice person and most people like me. It is sad that the parents feel I am not a good teacher, but that is their problem. I know that I am improving every day, in every way.' This is the effect (E) stage of the process. The completed exercise using these first two stages might look like this:

ABCDE

A = Activating event
Parents complain that teacher is not a good teacher and that their child is not making progress in the basic school subjects.

B = Belief
'I am no good as a teacher. I'll never be any good at this job. I am a failure.'

C = Consequence
'I feel so depressed.'

D = Disputation
'Where is the evidence that I am no good as a teacher apart from this one event? I have had many other successes. Even if I am not doing as well as I would like, I cannot be considered to be a failure as a person just because of one teaching criticism. That is being irrational.'

E = Effect
'I am sorry that these parents feel I am no good as a teacher, but I cannot be held responsible for their feelings. I am not perfect, but I am improving every day in every way. I am a good teacher. Other people like me and I like myself.'

Stage 3: Relaxation

Next it is necessary to learn how to relax the body and the mind. There are literally hundreds of ways to relax and many authors have written books on relaxation techniques. It does not matter which method of relaxation is used for this purpose of deconditioning so long as it works. For those who do not already have their own method, the following is a suggestion:

Sit in a comfortable armchair

Take off the shoes

Ensure all limbs are loose and limp

Fix eyes on a point on the ceiling just above normal eye level. This will be uncomfortable after a few seconds. Close eyes as soon as the strain is felt, allowing the head to fall onto the chest

Now think of each of your muscles and joints in turn and relax them, beginning with your toes and working up the body, via legs, sides, shoulders, neck, face, even the tongue, chest, stomach, and back down the legs to the toes.

Following this physical relaxation, observe the breathing, noting that it is automatic

Let 'it' breathe at the rate 'it' wants to; do not force breathing at all

Observe the breath in the abdomen as it breathes out
Say the word 'relax' at the same time as breathing out
Repeat the word 'relax for 10 times on every exhale.

At the end of this process, both mind and body should be sufficiently relaxed to be able to engage in the second part of this
deconditioning procedure.

Stage 4: Deconditioning the unconscious
This is the final stage in the treatment and is really self-hypnosis,
consisting mainly of what is often known as 'creative visualisation'. This, however, is more focused and involves seeing the
stressful event in the mind's eye while the eyes are closed. The
reason why it is important to visualise the event is that the
unconscious mind usually work in pictures. The stressful event
will be associated in the unconscious mind with negative emotions. The objective is to associate the event with pleasant emotions. Having first relaxed as outlined in Stage 3, the following
procedure should be adopted:

Picture in your mind's eye a scene where you know you are
    always relaxed.
This scene could be from the past or in the present.
Dwell on this scene for a few seconds, reliving the experience.
Slowly introduce the stressful scene, but this time also say
    aloud the positive statements about yourself you composed
    in Stage 2.
Return to visualising the relaxed scene and then back again to
    the stressful scene, saying again aloud the positive
    statements.

This procedure should be repeated until you are able to visualise
the stressful scene without feeling any negative emotions.

When next in the stressful situation you should be prepared to
feel the usual stressful emotion, but this time it will be lessened.
Once in the situation, you should think the 'self-talk' to yourself.
When at home, if possible immediately after the event, you
should repeat the whole treatment process. The second time you
meet the stressful situation, you should repeat the positive self-
talk and things will be easier. After a few sessions like this, you

will no longer feel any negative emotions when encountering the previously stressful situation. The old adage 'practice makes perfect' is certainly apt here.

What is meant by conditioning?

It is important to recognise that much of our behaviour is 'conditioned'; in other words, we have learned to think and to feel in certain ways out of habit. When two things regularly occur together, we are conditioned so that the appearance of one reminds us of the other, e.g. if somebody says 'man' we then think of 'woman'. So when we anticipate a stressful experience we think immediately of the feelings of anxiety. We previously associated the situation with anxiety and so become conditioned to interpret it negatively again. The event and the emotions have been 'paired', so that the appearance of the event automatically results in the negative emotion. The essence of stress management technique is to learn how to 'decondition' the mind so that the stressful event becomes associated not with the anxiety but with a pleasant emotion. This may seem simple enough, but unfortunately habits die hard. Habits generally sink into the *unconscious* mind and become automatic responses outside conscious control. Merely changing thinking is not sufficient to change the emotion without also considering that part of the mind known as the *unconscious*.

Rephrasing commonly held irrational beliefs

The challenging of irrational beliefs, forming the basis of Stage 2 (disputation stage), raises the issue of just how many irrational beliefs people tend to hold in life generally – beliefs that usually go unrecognised. As such they are a definite block to happiness and holding on to them can be a source of stress. As most people are unaware that they are holding irrational beliefs, such beliefs continue to be maintained and to adversely affect behaviour until one day, as a result of the stress suffered, they are challenged in a counselling relationship. Consider the following irrational beliefs together with their rephrasing into rational ones. The rephrasing of these beliefs, (set in bold type below), should result, firstly, in a 'watering down' of the emotion experienced and secondly, in a change of attitude. It is a change in attitude that is the main aim of RET.

I must be liked by everybody otherwise I cannot be happy
  – it is nice to be liked by everybody but not essential for happiness
When somebody says something bad about me I cannot stand it
  – it is too bad when this happens but some things have to be tolerated
I get anxious when I don't know what is happening
  – some uncertainties are inevitable in life and have to be faced
I have to do well or else I feel I am no good
  – some failure is inevitable in life as nobody excels at everything
I have to be able to resolve all the problems I face from time to time
  – nobody is totally in control of life's events
Life was meant to be fair and just
  – life is not always fair and some unfairness has to be tolerated
Life should always be free from pain
  – unpleasant things are inevitable now and again in life and have to be tolerated
We all need somebody to turn to when in trouble
  – it is nice to have this crutch but not essential for happiness
Other people usually cause my unhappiness
  – you cause your own unhappiness
My present problems are caused by my past life so I cannot do anything about them
  – this is untrue as human beings are motivated by the future if they allow themselves to be so

Summary

This chapter began by discussing the incidence of stress in teaching, its definition, its characteristics, and its effects. It then went on to show how stress in teaching can be managed and reduced. The principles of rational-emotive therapy were introduced and a self-help, four-stage process of stress management was outlined incorporating RET.

Revision questions

1. What do you understand by stress?
2. What is meant by 'deconditioning the unconscious'?
3. What is the main theoretical basis in RET?

Activity

Complete the following stress incident questionnaire to determine any stress levels:

During the last week have you	Yes	No	Don't know
1. Felt regularly irritable or bad tempered?			
2. Had difficulty in accepting any kind of criticism?			
3. Rarely laughed at anything?			
4. Worried over not meeting deadlines?			
5. Found you could not get on at all with some people?			
6. Not been able to say 'No' to some people?			
7. Not been able to lead the kind of life you want to lead?			
8. Felt taken for granted by anybody?			
9. Woken in the middle of the night thinking about a problem?			
10. Worried about balancing your finances?			
11. Not been able to engage in a hobby or leisure pursuit?			
12. Not been able to take regular exercise?			
13. Worried about things that might happen?			
14. Found it impossible to sit reading or doing nothing?			
15. Drunk, eaten, or smoked more than usual?			
16. Found it difficult to get off to sleep?			
17. Experienced headaches or other physical aches?			
18. Found it hard to get out of bed in the mornings?			
19. Forgotten to complete an important task?			
20. Felt disappointed with your work achievements?			

Score 2 points if you have answered Yes to each question, 1 point for answering Don't know, and 0 for answering No. The higher the score, the higher the stress level.

Score 0–10: You are very relaxed.
Score 11–20: You may need to reappraise your lifestyle.
Score 21–40: You are severely stressed and should give some priority to the Further Reading references in order to obtain more intensive help.

Further reading

Beck, A. T. (1989) *Cognitive Therapy and the Emotional Disorders*. Harmondsworth: Penguin.

Fontana, D. (1989) *Managing Stress*. London: Routledge.

LeShan, L. (1993) *How to Meditate: A Guide to Self Discovery*. London: Collins.

Chapter 7

The Seven-Day Self-Esteem Enhancement Programme

'*I cannot honestly say I am happy in my present job.*'

It might be thought that the above comment would be rare but judging from the recent survey conducted by the UK Opinion Research Corporation referred to earlier, it is not uncommon. In that survey, only 45 per cent of primary teachers considered that they were happy in their job.

The happiness concept

Most of us would know, if asked, whether we were happy or not, but if asked to define happiness different people are likely to give different definitions. Even the research workers in this field do not agree on definitions. For one person it could mean the total satisfaction of all their needs, whereas to another person of a more stoic, reflective temperament happiness might be defined as the giving up of all but the basic survival needs and the ability to be satisfied with only these few. Despite this problem of lack of consensus regarding definitions, there would be agreement that happiness is a pleasant feeling. Any emotion described in the opposite category would be defined as the absence of happiness. It seems that although we may not know for sure what happiness is, we certainly know it when we don't have it!

So how do we recognise happiness? Abraham Maslow, the eminent psychologist, referred to 'peak experiences' as one mark of the happy person (1954). These could include almost any form of human experience ranging from listening to a

Beethoven symphony to walking with a close friend along a deserted beach. One thing is clear from asking people 'What makes you happy?'. Whereas we can be sure about the state of happiness being a pleasant emotion, the sources of happiness are so varied that it is impossible to advise any individual on how to achieve it without having an intimate knowledge of the individual in question.

There is some agreement on happiness being an overall feeling as opposed to a temporary mood. This seems to have escaped those who campaign for the legislation of so-called 'soft drugs' on the grounds that they produce a 'happy state'. The same argument can be applied to the use of alcohol. What most of us mean by happiness is a long-term feeling of satisfaction with our lives in general. Maslow was referring, of course, to a specific happiness state rather than an overall feeling. If we accept the definition of happiness as an overall feeling of satisfaction with its accompanying pleasant emotions, the next question to be addressed is how we can set out to achieve happiness.

From the research outlined in this book, there is evidence that people can change their attitudes to themselves and so become happier people. Also, people can have control over the quality of their lives and their own self-esteem levels. Indeed, the theme of this book is the enhancement of self-esteem, and it can now be appreciated that without high self-esteem it is not possible to be a happy person as we have defined the term. This is because the low self-esteem person usually has a large measure of unpleasant feelings.

The concept of happiness has troubled philosophers for centuries but until recently has been neglected as a topic for research by psychologists. However, there have now been several research reports published on the concept. It is interesting that among the 'happiness programmes' published from time to time in the popular press the advice is more often than not that to be happy we must begin to 'like ourselves' – another way of saying that we should develop our self-esteem. Fortunately, these programmes are now beginning to receive the attention of serious research workers such as Fordyce (1977) in the USA, who designed a 14-point plan for the achievement of happiness. His list is as follows:

1. keep busy;
2. spend time socialising;
3. produce meaningful work;
4. be better organised;
5. stop worrying;
6. lower your aspirations;
7. develop positive thinking;
8. become present-orientated;
9. develop a healthy personality;
10. develop a social personality;
11. be yourself;
12. dismiss negative feelings;
13. work on close relationships;
14. place happiness as your priority in life.

It is interesting that this list contains many of the topics covered in this book which are considered to be necessary for the development of high self-esteem. We would be justified therefore in describing the following programme to develop high self-esteem as a programme also towards the achievement of happiness.

Positive affirmations

Having worked through the exercises and completed the strategies outlined throughout the book, you have now arrived at the climax of the book.

This involves a series of short activities to be completed on each of seven days as described on page 76. Day 7 consists of a number of positive affirmations to be repeated to yourself while in a state of relaxation. The affirmations have been selected as the essence of self-esteem enhancement and are explained below.

The past is behind me – my future is ahead
This principle confirms the attitude that the healthy person is motivated by the future and not by the past. If you dwell for long on past problems they will prevent you from changing. An effort has to be made to forget any past misfortunes. This is sometimes difficult but as thoughts of the past come into your head, you must tell yourself that it is not necessary to relive the past in order to change the present. We are all products of our

past experiences, combined with our constitutional make-up, but this need only be of historical interest: past experiences need no longer motivate us, the only reality is the present. This may need working at with an absolute refusal to think negative thoughts. If negative thoughts from the past do persist, tell your-self, 'I am a different person now.'

I am capable of determining my own destiny

During the earlier years of life we all depend on adults for survival. So we try to please them by behaving in ways which meet with their approval. We learn that if we behave in the opposite way, adults do not approve and it is unpleasant. So it is that we become 'conditioned' to behave in a manner the adults require. As we get older, we become less dependent on them but as a result of the conditioning we still tend to behave in the ways which brought us approval and to avoid the behaviour which brought us pain in childhood. Gradually, however, we become more independent and grow towards emotional maturity. We question our early conditioning and move towards being self-determinate. We recognise that we have choices. We can deter-mine the kind of person we would like to be.

I am a happy person and was meant to be happy

People are motivated naturally towards being happy. Unfor-tunately, some people have the misguided view that we must suffer in the short term in order to be happy in the long term. It may be necessary to work hard at a task in the short term in order to achieve a future success but even the most tedious of work should be enjoyed. If you are not enjoying what you are doing then – Stop it! Review it! Change it! You are meant to be happy!

My conscious and my unconscious minds are in harmony

Hypnosis has shown that we all have parts of our minds which contain ideas and memories from the past. These ideas may still motivate us. A common example of this is when we sometimes wake in the morning in a particular mood. When we say, 'I got out of bed on the wrong side this morning,' what has happened is that we have been dreaming and dreams are the expression of the unconscious. The content of the dream may remain in the unconscious but the feelings associated with the dream stay with us for a while. So we may feel in a bad mood but are not consciously aware of the reasons for it. The lesson is not to deny stress in our waking lives, as discussed in the previous chapter.

I do not have to depend on others for my self-esteem
Despite our need to be valued and approved of, life is full of disappointments and not everyone we meet will be nice to us all the time. While it is nice to be liked by everybody, this is not essential for happiness. Provided we are valued by those we love and we love ourselves, then we can learn to put up with some people who may not like us.

I am a likeable person and I like myself
The importance of positive 'self-talk' has already been discussed in connection with reducing stress. Any personal negative thoughts that might occur should always be dismissed immediately and substituted with this one.

The self-esteem enhancement programme

The following list of activities, to be completed over a seven-day period, brings together in one practical programme all the concepts of self-esteem enhancement discussed in previous chapters. The programme should provide a useful self-healing technique whenever you feel that teaching is beginning to be a strain. As such, it is recommended that it is used in conjunction with colleagues at regular intervals throughout a teaching year.

**The Seven-Day Self-Esteem
Enhancement Programme**

Day 1: Make a list of all your positive achievements, no matter how small, e.g. built a garden, planted a tree, won a race, obtained a teaching qualification, raised a family.

Day 2: Make a list of all your positive personal qualities, e.g. good-natured, helpful, courageous, good listener, good sense of humour.

Day 3: Complete the following sentences:
  (a) The thing I like best about myself is ....
  (b) I am proud of ....
  (c) I am happy when ....
  (d) I get pleasure from ....

Day 4: Recall a situation in which you either said or did something you now regret:
  (a) Talk to yourself positively as if counselling yourself, e.g. 'I am not really a bad person. The real me is OK despite what I said (or did).' Forgive yourself.
  (b) Decide what you wish you had done or said, close your eyes and imagine the situation again, but this time with you saying or doing the right thing.
  (c) Decide when next in that situation to act accordingly.

Day 5: Make plans for a future activity. It need not be anything dramatic, e.g. planting seeds in the garden, taking a holiday, seeing a film, visiting a friend.

Day 6: Indulge yourself. Select a favourite activity, e.g. walking, shopping for yourself, reading, having lunch with a friend.

Day 7: Do the relaxation activity outlined in Chapter 6 (pages 65–6). When relaxed repeat the affirmations:
The past is behind me – the future is ahead.
I am capable of determining my own destiny.
I am a happy person and was meant to be happy.
My conscious and unconscious minds are in harmony.
I do not have to depend on others for my self-esteem.
I am a likeable person and I like myself.

Exercises:
● Try to greet with a smile the first person you see each day.
● Share the programme with a colleague.

Chapter 8

Putting the job in perspective

The impression may have been given in this book that the teaching profession is in disarray and consists of thousands of stressed and disillusioned teachers. This may be so in some areas, but visit a school staffroom in many parts of the UK and Australia and there are teachers who are still enthusiastic and dedicated to the task of helping children develop their personalities and their attainments. These teachers are usually those who have learned how to cope with the inevitable pressures of the job and so have been able to maintain their self-esteem and also their sense of humour. They have been able to recognise the many pitfalls and potential stresses in teaching. Moreover, these teachers have been able to put the job in proper perspective and, although dedicated to the profession, they appreciate that there is a life also outside teaching. They know that life is not only about work: it is also about having fun.

Having fun

Teaching can be a very serious occupation. There are so many problems to be dealt with, often highly charged with emotion, particularly when having to deal with challenging behaviour. So to assert that teaching should be fun may sound a contradiction in terms. Of course, it is hard to be anything other than serious in the face of so many problems demanding attention but, even so, teaching should still be fun. It is all too easy in any profession to lose sight of the fact that having fun is an important characteristic of all living creatures, including teachers! The need to play which was so prominent in childhood remains dormant in all of us, although some of us seem to have forgotten how to express it. Teachers are often the last to cater for this need; their heavy workload quite realistically prevents many from having time to 'play'. It is essential in the interests of the happy teacher that time be put aside each week for some kind of recreational activity. It is all too easy to slip into the dull routine of 'work–bed–work' only broken by the need to shop and to cook.

In order to be able to see the funny side of anything, it is necessary first to be relaxed. The relaxed teacher will be able to laugh not only at comic events in the classroom but also at themselves. It is always possible to see the funny side of some aspects of teaching even if it is only minor events such as laughing at your own lack of ability to draw a straight line on the blackboard!

The ability to laugh at oneself is one characteristic of a true sense of humour and a mark of the mature personality. The philosopher Gratzalin comments on laughter:

> Everything done with laughter helps us to be human. It can be used to express an unending variety of emotions. It is based on guilt-free release of aggression, and any release perhaps makes us a little better and more capable of understanding one another, ourselves and life.

Teaching can be fun and teachers more than any other professional in modern society are in a privileged position to ensure that the children also have fun, so that both are more likely to find happiness.

Avoiding the stereotype

The danger of becoming a 'typical teacher' was referred to in Chapter 2 when discussing threats to self-esteem. Whenever a person becomes totally immersed in any kind of job there is always the risk of becoming a stereotype, e.g. a typical teacher or a typical psychologist. In these cases there is a one-sided attitude to life which Carl Jung, the great Swiss psychologist and philosopher, considered to be the source of some personality disorders (1923). To avoid this he advocated developing the whole personality. This process he termed 'individuation'. This cannot happen if a person concentrates wholly on a particular job such as teaching with no other outside interests. There will be parts of the personality which are neglected and Jung showed that unless all parts of the personality are used, they atrophy and leave the person feeling dissatisfied.

The lesson is clear: teachers are in danger of 'living the job'. As discussed earlier, the demands in teaching are infinite and as teachers, on the whole, are a conscientious lot, they readily take on extra work and often have little time for outside interests. The danger is that even if they make time for other things, they may move in a small social circle of other teachers and so tend to perpetuate the stereotype. Fordyce refers to the need to develop social contacts in general, but it is the need to develop contacts specifically outside the profession which is necessary if Jung's principle of Individuation is to be followed. In everyday terms, this amounts to having a 'rounded personality'.

The need to improve the image of the teacher

One area of stress and source of low self-esteem for many teachers is the erosion in society of the status of the profession of teaching. Not so long ago, teachers were regarded as professionals who had high status. The very words 'profession' and 'professional' conveyed status. These days the word 'professional' has itself become debased and has come to be used in so many different ways. It can refer to a person who performs a service to others or describe an excellent performance or simply mean the opposite of 'amateur' as in 'professional footballer'.

Accompanying this has been a questioning of authority in society in general. People no longer accept authority without question and children are no exception to this. Indeed, they are encouraged in school to speak up and to debate the issues of the day. Society has changed in this respect and is probably all the better for it. Workers question management, soldiers question their officers and children question adults. The teacher is no longer able to command the respect of children or their parents merely by being in the role of teacher. Respect has to be earned, just as it has to be earned in other walks of life, so teachers can no longer rely on an authoritarian role. This has had to be relinquished in favour of a more democratic one.

No longer are teachers able to take their professional status for granted. This, of course, has made some teaching more difficult than it used to be. Successful teaching depends today more on the personality of the teacher and less on an ascribed professional status in society. The high self-esteem teacher has no problem over earning respect and has no need to rely on their 'authority role' in order to try to gain the respect of the children in their charge. They earn respect and obedience through presenting to the children a human model of expertise in their subject and a cool fairness in dealing with any behavioural problems that may arise.

Ironically, teachers today often find their self-esteem under threat from sources that traditionally they were able to rely on for support. The present system of inspection is an example of this. Although the motives of the inspection system are impeccable, having as its aim the raising of standards in the profession, the inescapable fact is that so often it has reduced the self-esteem of teachers. Perhaps the time has come for the teaching profession to begin to regulate itself and to set up its own system of inspection within the profession – a self-governing body similar to that in the medical profession, the British Medical Association. How about the British Teaching Association? Experienced, highly qualified teachers could constitute this body and in so doing would gradually raise the status of the profession.

Teachers are overworked, they are underpaid and are often overtired. In addition, they are often blamed for the many ills in society. They need more recognition for the valuable job they do in helping children develop into responsible adults. Most teachers are dedicated to working in one of the most financially unrewarding and demanding of professions. We all need to value our teachers much more than we do. A society that undervalues its teachers undervalues its children.

The ancillary helper

There is one other developing trend in schools which could ease the burden of the teacher. This is the use of the ancillary helper. The status of the teacher is raised where a trained ancillary works under his or her direction and so leaves the teacher free of duties which do not demand their expertise, e.g. marking registers, organising outings, keeping records, and a host of administrative duties that teachers have traditionally been involved in but do not need to be. There is research showing that teachers spend on average only 30 per cent of the day in direct verbal interaction with children; the rest of the time is spent on administrative duties. The judicious use of the ancillary would leave the teacher free to pursue the multifarious roles of instructional expert, motivator, manager, counsellor, and above all leader with a high self-esteem model. In order for this to be successful there should be a proper training for ancillaries and an adequate pay structure appropriate to the work they do.

Summary

This chapter has focused on the need for teachers to place their work in proper context and have outside interests. It emphasised the need for teachers to ensure that they have fun. This chapter also referred to the valuable job teachers do despite the criticisms they receive and the pressures they encounter. Suggestions for improving the status of the profession are made. These include the setting up of a self-governing body and also the increased use of ancillaries.

Activity

Try answering the following questions:

1. Do you feel that society blames you for any of its ills?
2. How do you feel you can improve the image of the teacher?
3. Would it help to involve parents more?
4. What can you do in your classroom to maintain the status of the teacher?

Further reading

Bernard, M. B. (1990) *Taking the Stress out of Teaching*. Melbourne: Collins Dove.
Bridges, D. & Kerry, T. (1993) *Developing Teachers Professionally*. London: Routledge.
Dunham, J. (1992) *Stress in Teaching*. London: Routledge.

Appendix

Self-concept theory and the teacher

The need for a theory

There have always been teachers who have intuitively enhanced the self-esteem of children long before the research highlighted the relationship between self-esteem, achievement and behaviour. These teachers are probably of high self-esteem themselves and maintain their own self-esteem without any knowledge of self-concept theory. However, a knowledge of self-concept theory will help to sharpen up these skills. Although a knowledge of self-concept theory is not essential, it is advocated if teachers are to embark systematically on enhancing self-esteem, whether it be their own or that of their pupils. Similarly, an educational theory helps in the understanding of the process, so that techniques can be modified and even improved where necessary. As this book is meant to present a mainly practical programme for teachers, a brief overview only of self-concept theory is given here. For a fuller review of the concept, the reader should consult the further reading section at the end of the appendix.

The main theorists

The study of the Self as a psychological construct arrived in 1890 with William James' now famous book *Principles of Psychology*. Before James, the Self was considered to be a topic for the philosopher. After all, how could the Self be an object of study when it was the Self that was doing the studying; if the subject and the object of study were one and the same? William James attempted to resolve this dilemma by deliberately dividing the Self into the **me** – the contents of experience, and the **I** – the person experiencing the contents, i.e. the 'knower', and the 'known'. Further, James considered the Self as having four aspects:

1. The Spiritual Self.
2. The Material Self.
3. The Social Self.
4. The Bodily Self.

He represented self-esteem as a formula: self-esteem = Success divided by Pretensions. Using this formula, self-esteem could be enhanced by either increasing Successes or by reducing Pretensions (levels of aspirations). Whilst this was a useful beginning in the search for a working definition of self-esteem, a major criticism of it was that a person's own valued goals may not be the same as those of the society in which they live. For instance, a person may set out to be the best street cleaner in the town. This would be all right if the people whose opinions they cared about also valued the job, but what if the parents had academic aspirations for their child who wanted to be a street cleaner?

The Symbolic Interactionists

Later theorists such as Cooley (1902) with his 'Looking Glass Theory' took into account the influences of society and showed how people's self-worth depended to a much larger degree on the opinions of others than James had envisaged. There is no denying the influence of James, however; his work sparked off a flood of theories of the Self. Among those who followed Cooley, the Symbolic Interactionists led by Mead (1934) stand out. One of the distinguishing features of these theorists is the emphasis on the role of language in the developing self, which again, is dependent on social interaction. For the Symbolic Interactionists, the **I** part of the Self was there at the very beginning of life, and the process of development of the person paralleled the development of the **me**. This was akin to James's famous comment that development in the individual is one of a gradual 'differentiation' of the personality from what was originally in the infant just 'one big, blooming, buzzing confusion'.

The Behaviourists

Further developments in self-concept theory appeared to grind to a halt during the next couple of decades as Behaviourism became popular. There was no place for introspection in Behaviourism, which was concerned only with aspects of the person that could be measured and were amenable to empirical investigation. The Behaviourists considered the Self to be impossible to observe and so not a legitimate topic for the psychologists. Once again, the concept of Self was relegated to the realms of philosophy and regarded as not a respectable field of study for the psychologist.

Carl Rogers

It was not until the 1950s with the arrival of Carl Rogers that the Self once again became recognised as an important topic for psychology. Carl Rogers, arguably, has had the most significant influence on the development of self-concept theory, not least because he based his theories on actual case work with clients. Much of Rogers' work was suggested by previous self-concept theorists. However, there are three important notions in Rogers' theories which had not previously been suggested. His main thesis was that people are 'phenomenological' creatures. By this he meant that experiences are unique to the individual and so the Self could be thought of as a collection of experiences which are interpreted in a unique way. In other words, we can tell nothing about a person's state of mind merely by examining the events. It is a person's own interpretation of the events which are 'real'; an event that may appear to an observer to be traumatic may not be perceived as such by the person concerned.

A second important aspect of Rogers' theories is that people naturally have a need for positive regard, or self-esteem, both from others and from themselves. The third significant notion was that people have a need for self-consistency. Evidence for this comes from people who appear to cling to handicaps even where they may have an opportunity to surmount them. There are cases on record, for instance, where people born deaf have had the chance of an operation to correct the problem but have refused it. This need for consistency would also explain why it is not possible to enhance self-esteem overnight. In experiments conducted by the author into enhancing self-esteem of children, no measurable changes occurred before six months (Lawrence, 1972). Rogers would appear to be correct in his contention that the self resists change. A more obvious example of this is the low self-esteem child in the classroom who tears up his work despite having been praised for it by his teacher.

It is not only Rogers' contribution to self-concept theory which marks him as one of the outstanding psychologists of his era. His contributions in the general area of counselling are probably even greater achievements. He was the founder of the well-known counselling school known as Client-centred Therapy with its emphasis on non-directive counselling. It is through the work of Rogers that we can best understand how self-esteem develops and indeed how emotional disturbance can occur.

Implicit in Rogers' notion of the development of the self-concept is the idea that people strive for positive regard from others and they evaluate themselves accordingly. This was the view postulated by Cooley. However, Rogers went a stage further with this theory showing how the opinions of others eventually become 'internalised'. Emotional disturbance occurs when people continually receive views of themselves which are at odds with the 'real' self. Rogers called this process a 'distortion' of the self-concept. He said that distortion can also occur when there is incongruence between the self-image and the ideal self. In these cases, counselling would aim to help the client establish congruence between these two aspects of the Self.

Abraham Maslow

Another of Rogers' achievements is in his attempt to place his theories in the much wider context of the nature of humankind in general. Prior to Rogers, the Behaviourists had portrayed people rather like puppets reacting to their environment. Rogers showed how people are much more purposive than this and are potentially capable of determining their own destiny. Moreover, people appear to have a natural need for what he called 'self actualising'. This view was shared by Maslow, who was the first to draw attention to the phenomenon. Self-actualising was meant to describe the need we all have to achieve maturity through full expression of ourselves and the use of our talents. For Maslow, however, there is a hierarchy of needs with the need for self-actualising at the top. Lower down the scale are the basic needs, e.g. food, drink, sex, and self-preservation. It makes no sense, according to this view, to try to enhance self-esteem without ensuring that the basic needs are satisfied first. Both Maslow and Rogers asserted that people were capable of becoming self-determinate in their pursuit of self-actualising, a view which stands in marked contrast to that of the Behaviourists led by Skinner, and also the theories of Freud, earlier. For Maslow and Rogers – known also as proponents of the Humanistic School – people could be held responsible for their behaviour and are free to choose. However, they recognised also the influence of unconscious thought processes which sometimes had to be brought into consciousness before people were free.

Self-concept theory today

All the theorists discussed above have made an important contribution to self-concept theory, but unfortunately they have tended to operate in isolation from one another. This is one reason why, until recently, there was no real consensus on a definition of the self-concept. Happily, today, self-concept theory has drawn together the insights of past theorists so that a consensus has emerged. Most psychologists working today with self-concept theory would agree with the definitions outlined below.

Before considering these, it is useful to reflect on the fact that the self-concept, in common with many other notions in psychology, does not exist as an entity; it is a hypothetical construct postulated as an attempt to explain one aspect of human nature. As such, it is best thought of as an umbrella term incorporating three other constructs:

1. the self-image;
2. the ideal self;
3. the self-esteem.

1 Self-image

Self-awareness is a gradual process and goes on throughout life. People begin life relatively unconsciously and only gradually become aware of their unique characteristics as they 'bounce off the environment'. The development of the self-image therefore is primarily a conscious process. Physical awareness is probably the beginning of the process, with the newborn baby gradually becoming aware of the different parts of its body. Psychological awareness begins soon after this, with parents continually com-municating to their children the sort of people they are – 'You are a lovely baby', or, sadly, 'You are a cry baby.' Children begin to 'see themselves' as people with particular characteristics along dimensions which are bi-polar, e.g. clever–stupid, loveable–unloveable. This process continues as the child de-velops and begins to go around the neighbourhood meeting other people. The process begins in the family and continues throughout life, so that as adults people have become aware of a collection of personal attributes about themselves which we call **self-image**. Ask any adult who they are and they will probably give you a list such as 'a man, a father, tall, a kind person, a courageous person'. The more varied the experiences people have, the more aware they become of the themselves and so the richer this self-image is. It is interesting to reflect on the stage at which the newly qualified teacher begins to add the 'teacher' construct to their self-image. Student teachers invariably have a difficult time on their first teaching practice simply because they do not yet see themselves as teachers. With time they grow into the role of teacher and the concept 'teacher' becomes part of their self-image.

2 Ideal self

Alongside the development of the self-image, another process is taking place which again begins in infancy. Parents normally communicate to their children that certain behaviours and standards of achievement are desirable, e.g. it is nice to be clean and tidy, it is nice to be polite, and so on. As with the self-image, the process continues outside the family so that eventually the child learns that it is desirable to be clever, to be popular and to be able to excel on the sports field. Adults soon learn that having a successful career is particularly valued in our society. By the time the adult stage is reached, a host of values and aspirations have been acquired to form what we call the **ideal self**. Under normal circumstances, people gradually interject the values and standards of the society in which they live and work. They develop levels of aspiration and form goals for the future. Teachers aspire to be better teachers and often acquire further qualifications. It is interesting to observe that in the well-adjusted person, even where these goals have been attained, people seem to have a continued need for goals. In other words, their levels of aspiration are forever being pushed forward. It follows therefore that a discrepancy between the self-image and the ideal self is a natural phenomenon. In one sense therefore failure could be considered inevitable; it is the *attitude* towards failure which is of significance. It is this attitude towards the self-image/ideal self discrepancy which we call **self-esteem** and which is the subject of this book. A formal definition of self-esteem therefore would be the evaluation of the discrepancy between the self-image and the ideal self. Let us consider self-esteem in more detail and particularly with regard to the role of the teacher.

3 *The self-esteem*

If we accept our feelings of worth as being our attitudes towards the discrepancy between our self-image and our ideal self, it can be appreciated that for some people this discrepancy is too painful to bear. These are usually the people who have a strong need to achieve and to excel. Even the slightest failure for them is regarded as a disaster, whereas others with a similar discrepancy between their self-image and their ideal self may have a more relaxed attitude towards it. The former will feel failures and so will develop low self-esteem while the latter will not be so dramatically affected. Why should this be so?

Firstly, it is important to recognise that people can have in effect a number of 'self-esteems' dependent on how many aspects of their lives they care about. In some areas they can have high self-esteem but in others they may have low self-esteem. Some people are very confident in all situations while others seem to lack confidence in all situations. And there are those who appear to lack confidence in some situations but are confident in others. This is not at all unusual and is referred to in self-esteem theory as the *self-esteem hierarchy.*

At the top we have the *global* self-esteem, sometimes known as *general* self-esteem, and beneath we have what is known in the theory as *situation-specific* self-esteem. It is the global self-esteem which is the main area of interest and is the overall feeling of worth which we carry around all day and go to bed with at night. Nobody can feel successful in all situations and most of us have some feelings of inferiority with regard to specific situations, even though overall we feel all right.

However, if the specific situations in which we feel failures are situations which we regularly experience and which we regard as particularly important, very soon our global self-esteem is affected. Most adults are able to avoid those situations in which they perceive themselves to be failures and so preserve their global self-esteem. For instance, I feel inadequate playing golf. I can't hit the ball! However, my self-esteem is preserved as I do not consider this sport to be particularly important to me and as I find I am able to achieve success in other areas that I do regard as important I am able to preserve my global self-esteem.

Teachers who know that they are successes at teaching but perhaps not in some areas outside teaching similarly preserve their global self-esteem. It is their role as teachers which is the important one and it is the role of teacher which is seen today so often to be under threat (see Chapter 2 for a more specific discussion of this).

Origins of low self-esteem

There are a multitude of factors contributing to a person's level of self-esteem, beginning at birth and continuing throughout life. By the time a person is a fully-fledged adult, they have been subjected to numerous influences, both negative and positive. Admittedly, some teachers may enter the profession already with low self-esteem whilst there are others, probably the majority, who begin confident enough but, as already discussed, gradually develop low self-esteem as the pressures of the job increase.

It cannot be sufficiently emphasised that even where there may have been many negative influences which have contributed to low self-esteem, it is possible to reverse this trend and to develop high self-esteem. Influences of the past need no longer motivate.

The process of forming the self-concept began a long time ago in childhood when parents and other significant people in our lives first set us on the path of self-awareness. As we become adults we begin to form our own opinions of ourselves and so our self-concept, initially formed by others, is modified and extended. Our image of ourselves can end up being very different from that others have been giving us. However, most of us remain influenced to some degree by our childhood experiences and in some cases it can take a considerable effort before we are able to discard those early childhood influences. How many of us, for instance, still feel vaguely ill at ease when confronted with an authority figure?

Eventually, with increased awareness of self and with appropriate experiences it is possible to become self-determinate. There is little doubt however that some people have irrational feelings of inadequacy which can be traced back to early childhood experiences. It is important to emphasise that although low self-esteem may have been formed in early childhood, we can change. Moreover, the evidence from counselling studies shows that it is not necessary to have to 'unravel' these experiences to do so. We can start with the here and now. We *will* continue to be influenced by our early experiences unless we look to the future and plan future goals for personal development.

The need for self-esteem

The need for self-esteem is probably the most important need we have in our kind of society. Textbooks on psychology usually list the basic needs of hunger, thirst, sex, and self-preservation as the most important human needs. However, these are relatively easily satisfied in contrast to the need for self-esteem.

People can be seen in all walks of life striving to maintain self-esteem – parents in conflict with children, people in conflict with each other, teachers in conflict with administrators, workers in conflict with management in industry, nations in conflict with each other. In effect they are all saying the same thing – 'Respect me.'

Teachers are no exception and with the ever increasing pressures on the profession their self-esteem today is more than ever at risk. Teachers' self-esteem is at risk not only from without but also as a result of the kind of personality teachers generally appear to have. In a survey of differences in personality among the professions conducted some years ago by Professor R. B. Cattell, it was concluded that teachers were more 'tender-minded' than other professionals and more inclined to be sensitive to criticism (1965).

It is always dangerous to generalise and certainly not all teachers would fit the stereotype described by Cattell. Even so, his research is food for thought. In theoretical terms, it is fair comment that the discrepancy between the teacher's self-image and ideal self is widening as the demands on the profession are increasing. The end product is that teachers often blame themselves for this and so put their self-esteem at risk. The message is clear. If teachers are to maintain their self-esteem in today's climate then they need to care more for themselves and learn how to cope with the inevitable increase in pressures.

The Self as a motivator

From the foregoing account of the development of self-esteem it should be clear that the Self is a learned concept and a product of experience. However, the Self is not only formed by experiences; it also determines experiences. In other words, the Self is a motivator and people are motivated to behave in ways which fit in with their self-concept. So, for instance, the person who sees themself as an intellectual will tend to seek intellectual pursuits; the person who perceives themselves as a physical athlete will be motivated towards sporting pursuits.

Moreover, we tend to feel more secure when behaving in ways that we perceive as fitting in with our self-concept. We feel decidedly insecure if suddenly thrust into a situation which does not fit our image of ourselves. The student teacher invariably feels insecure when having to stand in front of a class of children for the first time. Whenever a person embarks on a new career or takes on a new role, there is always a settling-in period of relative insecurity. These feelings gradually disappear as the self-concept is modified. It is important that student teachers are made aware of this beforehand in order to prevent undue anxiety over what is after all an inevitable and only temporary feeling of insecurity.

Summary

- Self-concept consists of self-image, ideal self and self-esteem.
- Self-image is a person's perception of their mental and physical characteristics.
- Ideal self is formed initially through adopting the standards and values of 'significant others'.
- With normal development these values are modified and adults set their own standards.
- Self-esteem is a person's evaluation of the discrepancy between their self-image and ideal self.
- Self-concept is a motivator.
- Self-concept is resistant to change.
- Research indicates a consistently positive correlation between self-esteem, academic achievement, behavioural difficulties, locus of control and general happiness.
- The person with high self-esteem is confident, relaxed and eager to take on new challenges.
- Confidence is self-esteem in practice and has two aspects:
  (i) confidence in abilities
  (ii) confidence in personality.

Further reading

Burns, R. (1982) *Self-Concept Development and Education*. Sydney: Holt, Rinehart and Winston.

James, W. (1890) *Principles of Psychology, Vol. 1*. New York: Henry Holt.

Lawrence, D. (1973) *Improved Reading Through Counselling*. London: Ward Lock.

Maslow, A. H. (1954) *Motivation & Personality*. New York: Harper and Row.

Rogers, C. R. (1951) *Client Centred Therapy*. Boston: Houghton Mifflin.

Skinner, B. F. (1953) *Science & Human Behaviour*. New York: Macmillan.

Thomas, J. B. (1980) *The Self in Education*. Slough: NFER.

Select bibliography

Allport, G. W. (1938) *Personality: A Psychological Interpretation*. London: Constable.

Argyle, M. (1987) *The Psychology of Happiness*. Harmondsworth: Penguin.

Argyle, M. (1997) *Psychology of Interpersonal Behaviour*. London: Penguin.

Bandura, A. (1977) *Social Learning Theory*. New Jersey: Prentice Hall.

Beck, A. T. (1989) *Cognitive Therapy and the Emotional Disorders*. Harmondsworth: Penguin.

Bernard, M. B. (1990) *Taking the Stress out of Teaching*. Melbourne: Collins Dove.

Berne, E. (1967) *Games People Play*. London: Andre Deutsch.

Branden, N. (1995) *Six Pillars of Self-Esteem*. London: Bantam.

Bridges, D. and Kerry, T. (1993) *Developing Teachers Professionally*. London: Routledge.

Burnard, P. (1994) *Counselling Skills for Health Professionals*. London: Chapman and Hall.

Burns, R. (1979) *The Self-Concept Theory, Measurement, Development and Behaviour*. London: Longman.

Burns, R. (1982) *The Self-Concept Development in Education*. London: Holt, Rinehart and Winston.

Cattell, R. B. (1965) *Scientific Analysis of Personality*. Harmondsworth: Penguin.

Charles, C. (1995) *Building Classroom Discipline*. Harlow: Longman.

Claxton, G. (1989) *Being a Teacher*. London: Cassell.

Cole, M. and Walker, S. (eds) (1989) *Teaching and Stress*. Milton Keynes: Oxford University Press.

Combes, A. (1965) *The Professional Education of Teachers*. Boston: Allyn and Bacon.

Cooley, C. H. (1902) *Human Nature and the Social Order*. New York: Charles Scribner's Sons.

Doring, A. (1993) Why me? Stress and the deputy. *British Journal of In-Service Education*, **19** (3), pp. 18–22.

Dunham, J. (1992) *Stress in Teaching*. London: Routledge.

Ellis, A. (1979) *Theoretical and Empirical Foundations of Rational-Emotive Therapy*. Monterey, Calif.: BrooksCole.

Erikson, E. (1959) *Identity and the Life Cycle*. New York: IUP.

Eysenck, H. (1977) *Psychology is About People*. Harmondsworth: Penguin.

Eysenck, M. (1994) *Happiness: Facts and Myths*. Hove: Lawrence Erlbaum.

Fontana, D. (1989) *Managing Stress*. London: Routledge.

Fordyce, M. W. (1977) Development of a programme to increase personal happiness. *Journal of Counselling Psychology,* **24**, pp. 511–21.

Gordon, T. (1974) *Teacher Effectiveness Training.* New York: Wyden.

Hall, E. and Hall, C. (1988) *Human Relations in Education.* London: Routledge.

Hall, E., Woodhouse, D. A. and Wooster, A. D. (1988) Reducing teacher stress. *British Journal of In-Service Education,* **14**(2), pp. 72–4.

Harris, T. (1979) *I'm OK – You're OK.* London: Pan Books.

Hopson, B. and Scally, M. (1981) *Life Skills Teaching.* London: McGraw Hill.

James, W. (1890) *Principles of Psychology.* New York: Henry Holt.

Jenks, C. (1996) *Childhood.* London: Routledge.

Jung, C. G. (1923) *Psychological Types.* New York: Harcourt Brace.

Lawrence, A. (1998) *Interagency Collaboration in the Management of Child Sexual Abuse.* Unpublished PhD Thesis, University of Plymouth.

Lawrence, D. (1973) *Improved Reading Through Counselling.* London: Ward Lock.

Lawrence, D. (1982) Development of a self-esteem questionnaire. *British Journal of Educational Psychology,* **51**(1), pp. 48–54.

Lawrence, D. (1998) *Enhancing Self-Esteem in the Classroom.* London: Paul Chapman Publishing.

McIntyre, T. C. (1984) The relationship between locus of control and teacher burn-out. *British Journal of Educational Psychology,* **54**, pp. 235–8.

Maslow, A. (1968) *Motivation and Personality.* New York: Harper and Row.

Mead, G. H. (1934) *Mind, Self and Society.* Chicago: University of Chicago Press.

Mo, K. W. (1991) Teacher burn-out: relations with stress, personality and social support. *Educational Journal,* **19**, pp. 3–11.

O'Connor, P. R. and Clarke, V. A. (1990) Determinants of teacher stress. *Australian Journal of Teacher Education,* **34**, pp. 41–51.

Palmer, S. (1981) *Role Stress.* Englewood Cliffs: Prentice Hall.

Phares, E. J. (1976) *Locus of Control in Personality.* New Jersey: General Learning Press.

Pratt, J. (1978) Perceived stress among teachers. *Educational Review,* **30** (1), pp. 3–14.

Rogers, C. R. (1967) *On Becoming a Person.* London: Constable.

Rogers, C. R. (1975) Empathy: An unappreciated way of being. *The Counselling Psychologist,* **5** (2), pp. 2–9.

Rogers, W. A. (1992) *Supporting Teachers in the Workplace.* Milton, Queensland: Jacaranda.

Rotter, B. (1982) *The Development and Applications of Social Learning Theory: Selected Papers.* Brattleboro: V. T. Praeger.

Rowland, V. and Birkett, K. (1992) *Personal Effectiveness for Teachers.* Hemel Hempstead: Simon and Schuster.

Seligman, M. (1991) *Learned Optimism.* London: Random House.

Selye, H. (1976) *The Stress of Life.* New York: McGraw Hill.

Skinner, B. F. (1953) *Science and Human Behaviour.* New York: Macmillan.

Stevens, R. (ed.) (1995) *Understanding the Self.* London: Sage.

Thomas, J. B. (1980) *The Self in Education.* Slough: NFER.

Weiner, B. *et al.* (1996) *Perceiving the Causes of Success and Failure.* New Jersey: General Learning Press.

Wilson, B. (1996) *The Assertive Teacher.* Aldershot: Arena.

Index